LEWIS & CLARK

PART I

FROM JEFFERSON'S PARLOR TO THE GREAT PLAINS

BRAD PHILLIPS

THE WAYSIDE BOOKSHOP

Published by:
Apricot Press
Box 1611
American Fork, Utah
84003

books@apricotpress.com
www.apricotpress.com

ISBN 1-885027-25-7

Printed in the United States of America

Cover: "Lewis and Clark Expedition in 1804"
Dean Cornwell
Oil on Canvas, ca. 1955
Courtesy of the Montana Historical Society
Gift of the New York Life Insurance Co.

Introduction

This is a book filled with stories. I have tried to provide the names, dates, places, and other facts as necessary, but my ultimate goal is to tell the story. You may not care that the expedition set out from Pittsburgh on August 31, 1803, at 10:00 A.M. I know I don't. But I was shocked to learn that Lewis was nearly responsible for a woman's death just a few hours later.

The basic plot is simple. Jefferson sent Lewis and Clark across the continent to see what was there. They picked up Sacajawea along the way, made it to the Pacific, and then came back. The drama in this story comes not from the outcome—we all know they made it—but from the journey. The men of the Lewis and Clark expedition experienced an adventure that will never be repeated. They were the first white men to see the Great Falls of the Missouri, the first ones to catch a prairie dog, the first to hike across the Rocky Mountains. Their exploits impressed even the Indians. While the men were shooting the Columbia River rapids, some of the tribes actually gambled on where and when the party would wreck their canoes, and then waited downstream so they could salvage their belongings. Likewise, the Indians never failed to amaze the captains. While the expedition was at winter camp in North Dakota, two Mandans were separated on a hunting expedition and forced to spend a sub-zero night outdoors. Such an ordeal would have surely killed any member of the expedition, yet the Indians survived with only minor injuries. Clark wrote that the Mandans could "bare more Cold than I thought it possible for man to indure."

As the previous quote indicates, Clark's spelling and capitalization are inventive. I have not made any effort to correct him. Fixing my own mistakes was enough of a challenge. Being a middle-aged white guy, I also tend to use terms like Indian and American that are not technically accurate but very convenient for describing the native inhabitants of North America and citizens of the United States, respectively. No offense is intended. Writing this book has enlarged my respect for both groups.

Most of the stories in these books are taken from the journals kept by the men of the expedition. I have also consulted modern authors and their interpretations. Occasionally, I will venture an opinion that cannot be proven from the historical texts. In that case, I will use a word like "probably" or "likely" so you will know I am speculating.

This series is written, more or less, as a chronological account of the expedition. However, there are some fascinating stories that do not fit neatly into such a description. Every other chapter advances Lewis and Clark along the trail. In between, I will take a look backwards, forwards, or sideways to discuss something that doesn't fit directly into a straight-line narrative. For example, Chapter 9 explains why Napoleon gave Jefferson such a great deal on the Louisiana Territory and Chapter 4 explains why expanding the size of the United States was so critical to many of the Founding Fathers. Like Lewis and Clark, who were sometimes forced by the Missouri River to take a meandering path to their destination, we will get to the end eventually.

- Brad Phillips

Contents

Illustrations

Letter written by Thomas Jefferson to Andre Michaux, January 23, 1793.
Library of Congress, Manuscript Division.

Chapter 1
A Secret Meeting

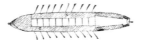

"Mr. Jefferson and several other gentlemen are much interested, and think they can procure a subscription sufficient to insure one thousand guineas as a compensation to any one who undertakes the journey and can bring satisfactory proof of having crossed to the South Sea."

— June 20, 1792, Letter from Caspar Wistar of the American Philosophical Society to botanist Moses Marshall, describing Jefferson's plans to explore to the Pacific.

A casual observer would never guess that Andre Michaux was a French secret agent. Technically, he was a botanist and a good one. His book, Flora Boreali-Americana, was widely read for decades. But being a botanist in the 18th Century was not all done in the safety of laboratories and universities. When Michaux traveled to the Middle East on a botanical expedition he was attacked by bandits, stripped naked, and left to die on a mountain pass. He survived that adventure and compiled a French-Persian dictionary while nursing himself back to health.

Upon his return to France in 1785, the director of royal parks and gardens sent Michaux across the Atlantic to explore the trees of the newly formed United States in the hope that specimens could be transplanted in France and used for ship timbers. Three weeks after he landed in New York, shipments of trees, seeds, cranberries, and sweet potatoes were on their way back to France. Michaux then set out to explore and catalog the botany of the new continent. He covered more of the United States than any native citizen. From the swamps of Florida to the northern tundra of Canada, and west through the Northwest Territories, Michaux observed and recorded and collected. By necessity, he became one of America's most skilled frontiersmen.

Michaux's expertise in botany and mountaineering made him the ideal candidate to lead an American expedition to the Pacific Ocean. In 1792, Secretary of State Thomas Jefferson recruited Michaux for that purpose, passing over his young neighbor Meriwether Lewis, who implored Jefferson to be included. The American Philosophical Society collected $128.25 to finance this transcontinental expedition, of which almost half came from Jefferson, Washington, and Hamilton. Woefully under-funded, Michaux set out for the Pacific Ocean with explicit instructions from Jefferson to "find the shortest & most convenient route of communication between the US. & the Pacific ocean, within the temperate latitudes, & to learn such particulars as can be obtained of the country through which it passes, it's productions, inhabitants & other interesting circumstances."

Jefferson didn't realize that Michaux had instructions of his own from the new French ambassador, Citizen Edmond Charles Edouard Genet. On his way to the Pacific he was to recruit American and French citizens and attack Spanish possessions along the Mississippi. This secret mission brought Michaux face to face with one of the great heroes of the Revolutionary War; a man second only to General

George Rogers Clark, Revolutionary War hero and older brother of William Clark. Painting from the Library of Congress, Prints and Photographs Division, LC-USZ61-140.

Washington in using strategy and deception to defeat a superior enemy. He was General George Rogers Clark, older brother of William Clark.

In 1777, at the age of 25, General Clark had been commissioned a Lieutenant Colonel by the Virginia General

As America's first President, Washington carefully avoided entanglement in European affairs. Here, he meets the new ambassador from France, Citizen Edmond Charles Edouard Genet. Painting from the Library of Congress, Prints and Photographs Division, LC-USZ62-100719.

Assembly and received authority to build a force to defend Kentucky from the Indians and the British. Clark led a small force stealthily up the Ohio River to the fort town of Kaskaskia, which they captured without a single shot on July 4, 1778. Clark then moved quickly against the British stronghold in Vincennes. He marched his force through flooded plains in the middle of winter and forced a surrender after three days. He didn't lose a single man. The capture of these posts effectively pushed the border of British control up to the Great Lakes, which was formalized by the Treaty of Paris at the end of the Revolutionary War.

During the campaign, Clark had assumed responsibility for many of the debts incurred by his army, trusting vainly in Jefferson's advice to "safely confide in the Justice & Generosity of the Virginia Assembly." The result was that General Clark had been all but ruined financially. Yet if the Virginians no longer had any use for Clark, the French certainly did. With Michaux as a possible go-between, Clark promised Genet that he could rally his old comrades to this new cause and quickly overrun the poorly defended Spanish garrisons. The French responded by making him a "major-general of the Independent and Revolutionary Legion of the Mississippi." Once word of the plot leaked to the Spanish authorities, something near panic set in. The Spanish governor in New Orleans, Baron Carondelet, felt certain that "all Louisiana will fall into their hands with the greatest rapidity." He even feared the loss of Mexico.

Now Michaux was on his way to meet with Clark in Kentucky and set the plot into motion, courtesy of three Founding Fathers. Technically, the plot was not treasonous. There was no law against either Clark or Michaux recruiting Americans to attack a foreign country at peace with the United States. No legislator had foreseen the need. The plot was, however, a very dangerous idea from the U.S. perspective. If a former American general were to lead a group of Americans in a campaign to take Spanish territory for the French, America would be clearly meddling in the affairs of Europe—a policy that was anathema to President Washington and would have likely led to war. And the fledgling American republic was in no position to fight a war with any European power.

The details of the secret meeting between Andre Michaux and George Rogers Clark, sometime in the fall of 1793, are unknown. They likely discussed the number of men they would recruit, how they would be deployed, and how Clark would be rewarded. He had already spent $5,000 of borrowed money buying supplies for the troops. After his experience with the Virginian Assembly, he should have known better. Michaux was truly a botanist at heart, and probably questioned Clark about the unique trees and plants he had discovered in his travels. He would also have wanted to know about the Indians he might encounter as he proceeded west to the Pacific.

Before the French plan could take effect and at the insistence of nervous Spanish diplomats, President Washington stepped in. Secretary of State Jefferson not so subtly informed Genet that General Clark would probably be hanged if he participated in the French scheme but "except for that I did not care what insurrections should be excited in Louisiana." Genet got the message, and so did Clark, although only four years later the General was scheming with the Canadians to attack Spanish New Mexico. The French never paid him though they let him keep his title. Genet was recalled as ambassador at Washington's insistence. Fearing that he might lose his head like so many of his countrymen if he returned to France, Genet pleaded to remain in America as a private citizen. His request was generously allowed. The Michaux expedition to the Pacific ended at General Clark's house. He stayed a few more years in the United States to complete his botanical work and returned to France.

Thus ended another of Jefferson's attempts to send an expedition to the Pacific. It was a noble venture, fulled with perils from competing European powers, hostile Indians, and most of all, nature. In 1793, the timing was not yet right. Fortunately for the United States, Jefferson would try again.

Reproduced from the original painting by Rembrandt Peale through the courtesy of the New-York Historical Society.

Photomechanical print, created/published [between 1890 and 1940(?)]. This print is a reproduction of the 1805 Rembrandt Peale painting of Thomas Jefferson held by the New-York Historical Society.

Chapter 2
Jefferson's Inauguration Day

"But every difference of opinion is not a difference of principle. We have called by different names brethren of the same principle. We are all Republicans, we are all Federalists. If there be any among us who would wish to dissolve this Union or to change its republican form, let them stand undisturbed as monuments of the safety with which error of opinion may be tolerated where reason is left free to combat it."

— From Jefferson's first inaugural address

When Thomas Jefferson took the oath of office as the third President of the United States on March 4, 1801, the land that would eventually become the United States was largely unknown to both Europeans and Americans. Although Spain, France, England, Russia, and the United States had asserted sovereignty in various parts of North America, they all knew practically nothing about the vast territory they claimed to possess. Jefferson himself, who was certainly one of the most intelligent and educated men of his day, believed that:

9

• The Blue Ridge Mountains of Virginia might be the highest on the continent.

• Somewhere along the Great Plains, there existed a mountain of pure salt over a mile long.

• The upper Missouri still contained prehistoric creatures like the mammoth and the ground sloth.

• All the great rivers of the West—the Missouri, Columbia, Colorado, and Rio Grande—flowed from a single high point.

• Most importantly, Jefferson believed that, although there was no direct "Northwest Passage," a low portage between the Missouri and Columbia might make transcontinental water traffic practical.

Jefferson had another farfetched notion that would turn out to be much more accurate: that someday the colonies would expand westward and create one country from ocean to ocean. In 1801, the discovery of mammoths would have seemed the better bet. From our vantage point in the 21st Century, the creation of the United States seems almost inevitable. At the turn of the 18th Century, it was neither inevitable nor particularly likely.

Jefferson's democratic vision, as outlined in the Declaration of Independence, was off to a rocky start. Distrust between the various states and regions resulted in a central government so constrained that it could barely raise enough tax revenue to fulfill its meager responsibilities. In 1787, after only a decade of existence, the new republic required a new Constitution to maintain a central government. After months of negotiations, an uneasy compromise was reached between the states. The new Constitution might still have failed if not for George Washington. Washington was the one man who had earned the respect and trust of delegates from all the states. He was the indispensable choice to be President. He was also one of the few leaders in world history with the character to

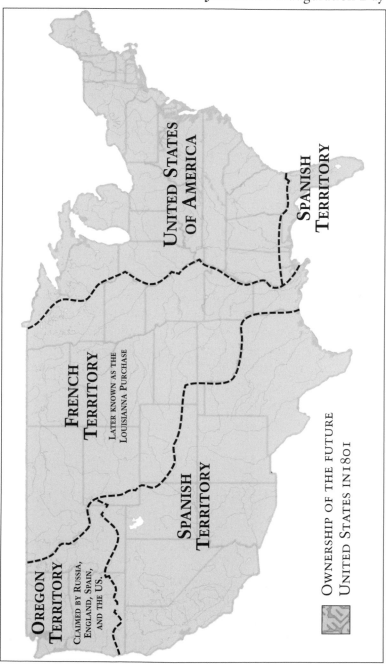

UNITED STATES
OF AMERICA

SPANISH
TERRITORY

FRENCH
TERRITORY

LATER KNOWN AS THE
LOUISIANNA PURCHASE

SPANISH
TERRITORY

OREGON
TERRITORY

CLAIMED BY RUSSIA,
ENGLAND, SPAIN,
AND THE U.S.

OWNERSHIP OF THE FUTURE
UNITED STATES IN 1801

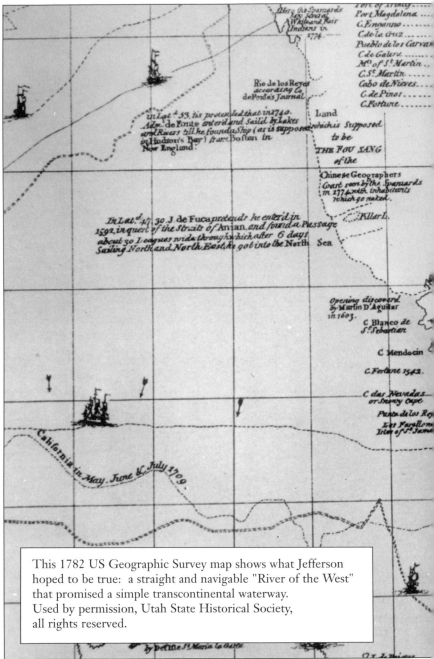

This 1782 US Geographic Survey map shows what Jefferson
hoped to be true: a straight and navigable "River of the West"
that promised a simple transcontinental waterway.
Used by permission, Utah State Historical Society,
all rights reserved.

voluntarily relinquish power to a democratically elected successor.

The new American nation also faced serious threats from abroad. Great Britain was still smarting from their defeat in the Revolutionary War. The British wanted to be sure that their former colonies did not impinge on their lucrative fur trade in the north and west. At the same time, the British kept a wary eye on their long-time foes in France. In 1800, the French had acquired the Louisiana Territory from Spain by the secret Treaty of San Ildefonso. Napoleon intended to create a French New World Empire centered in Hispaniola (modern-day Haiti) and supplied by trade goods from the Mississippi Valley. He planned to send his brother-in-law to Hispaniola to put down the slave rebellion and re-establish the French Empire. Napoleon's re-energized ambitions for France constituted a serious threat to President Jefferson's dream of a transcontinental American state. Jefferson had already stated that "there is on the globe one single spot, the possessor of which is our natural and habitual enemy. It is New Orleans, through which the produce of three eighths of our territory must pass to market." Somehow, Jefferson needed to find a way to make on American claim on possessions that were integral to both British and French plans for the region; and he had to do this without provoking a war.

The idea of a man walking away from power was incomprehensible to the Europeans. Just before President Washington's second term was set to expire, England's King George III—the king Washington defeated during the Revolutionary War—observed of his former enemy, "If George Washington goes back to his farm he will be the greatest character of his age." Napoleon, never one to shrink from power, grumbled about Washington's self-sacrificing example. While Napoleon was in exile and expected to stay out of politics for the good of France, he angrily claimed that his enemies wanted him "to be another Washington."

In Washington's farewell address he articulated a foreign policy strategy that was closely followed by Adams and Jefferson. In short, the strategy was to remain neutral in European affairs at all costs so that the United States would have time to grow into a nation strong enough to defend itself. The country was too young and too weak too attempt another war right after the Revolution. Since then, the new nation had walked a delicate tightrope between the great powers of Britain and France. Fortune and good leadership intervened on several occasions to stave off a second, and likely disastrous, war with both the British and the French.

The United States also faced internal threats. While the Founding Fathers worried about a rift between the large and small states or between the North and South over slavery, the first major conflict came between the East and West. The cause was Secretary of the Treasury Alexander Hamilton's excise tax on whiskey. This form of revenue disproportionately affected settlers in the western states. Whiskey was one of their chief manufactured goods and they had little hard currency with which to pay the tax. Furthermore, the federal government was doing nothing, as the settlers saw it, to protect them from the Indians and the British. The result was the Whiskey Rebellion of 1794. Tax collectors were shot at and even tarred and feathered. Their homes were burned. This insurrection put Washington in an awkward position. In 1776, he had risked his life to oppose British tax policies almost identical to the ones he was now pledged to enforce. The Westerners even mimicked the arguments of the Founding Fathers, suggesting that just as the Atlantic Ocean precluded British rule in the colonies, the Appalachians similarly formed a natural barrier necessitating two separate countries. If the western states were to be ruled by a distant government, the most logical location would not be New York but New Orleans, through which all of their trade goods flowed. Washington also had a personal investment in the western territories that created a considerable conflict of interest. He was one of the largest land speculators in the United States, owning tens of thousands of acres in a region of the country that suddenly seemed uninterested in belonging to the union. Washington wasted little time in raising an army to put down the Whiskey Rebellion. By the time the army had assembled and marched to Pittsburgh, the rebellion was over. The leaders had fled to Louisiana Territory and the farmers who had so bravely fought off lone revenue officers had no desire to fight an army. Still, a message was sent. Without political--or even military--attention, the western states might well form their own country or join their more natural allies in Louisiana.

Jefferson's Vice-President Aaron Burr understood the political dynamics in the West. Spain was a fading power, struggling to maintain control of their New World possessions. The young United States would have difficulty governing any territory west of the original colonies. Burr envisioned a great country carved out of the center of the continent. With a little British help he could raise an army, quickly seize control of all Louisiana and Mexico, and make his capital in New Orleans. Burr's partner in the scheme, General James Wilkinson, changed his mind and denounced Burr to U.S. authorities. Burr was quickly taken into custody. In 1807, during Jefferson's second term, his former Vice-President would stand trial for treason. Only Chief Justice John Marshall's narrow interpretation of the treason statute saved Burr from hanging.

So Thomas Jefferson came to the new President's House in the new capital of Washington D.C. with a formidable set of challenges to his dream of a transcontinental nation. Britain and France were both eager to expand their empires at the expense of the United States and the U.S. military was in no condition to oppose them. Of course, the Native Americans felt no need to formally claim land they had inhabited for centuries. They could easily join with France or Britain or attack U.S. settlements on their own. The new states of the west would be just as happy to create their own nation or join a foreign power in Louisiana. In addition, Jefferson's hold on power was tenuous at best. His inauguration likely marked the first time in world history

In 1801, Jefferson—and Meriwether Lewis--lived in the "President's House." Eleven years later, war would break out again with Britain, and a raiding party would invade the President's House, help themselves to a dinner Dolly Madison had prepared for guests, and then start a fire. To repair the damage, a new coat of paint was required, and the building then came to be known as "The White House."

that political power had been transferred peacefully from one ruling faction to an opposing faction by a democratic election. Jefferson's Republicans had narrowly defeated Adams' Federalists, but at a high cost both personally and politically. The Federalists were furious at Jefferson's tactics and his policies. Would their opposition make the republic ungovernable? The one man whose integrity and respect had held the republic together—George Washington--had been dead for two years. Jefferson was on his own. All of these problems faced the new President, plus one more: science.

Between 500 B.C. and 1801, relatively little improvement had been made in the way men communicated, transported goods and people, grew their crops, and treated illnesses. As Stephen Ambrose explains in Undaunted Courage, nothing moved faster than the speed of a horse. No goods, no letter, no person, no idea moved faster than a horse. Clearly, no President could govern a man in California, over 100 horse-days away. It is difficult to understand why Jefferson believed a transcontinental United States could ever be viable. The most powerful nations in Europe were about the size of his home state of Virginia. With the exception of a decentralized and often chaotic Russia no successful nation-state of that size had existed since the Roman Empire. In fact, horsepower and horse-speed had been the standard since Greek and Roman times. However, Jefferson was not looking to the past. His home in Monticello is filled with new inventions. His journals are filled with new ideas. He anticipated air travel and automobiles by over a century. Perhaps that inventor's mindset helped him look beyond what had been for the last 2,500 years and anticipate what might occur in the next sixty. By the time Abraham Lincoln took office in 1860, steamboats and railroads had nearly rendered the horse obsolete as a means of transporting cargo and the telegraph had made the transmission of information almost instantaneous. Within another four decades the creation of Jefferson's transcontinental nation would be complete.

But in 1801, someone from the United States first needed to visit the unknown territory. The ideal candidate would need to be competent in botany, zoology, astronomy, and cartography. He would need to be brave, yet diplomatic. He would need to be a leader of men. He would need to be a Republican so Jefferson could trust him. He would need to be personally trained by Jefferson to accomplish this very difficult mission. There were very few men who fit this description. Fortunately, one of them was on his way to see the President.

Chapter 3

The Foundation of the Expedition

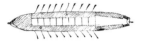

"I think this is the most extraordinary collection of talent, of human knowledge, that has ever been gathered at the White House-with the possible exception of when Thomas Jefferson dined alone."

—John F. Kennedy, regarding his high-powered group
of cabinet advisors

Today, if the President of the United States chose as his personal secretary an old friend of the family, still in his mid-twenties, with hardly any formal education, and spelling problems too numerous to discuss, a scandal would erupt immediately. Fortunately for Meriwether Lewis, in 1801, the President could manage his office with wide latitude. This was also fortunate for Jefferson who, in keeping with his Republican principles, ran the President's House with much less formality than Washington or Adams.

The first page from Jefferson's Secret Message to Congress Regarding the Lewis & Clark Expedition (1803).

National Archives and Records Administration

When visitors came to see Jefferson, whether it was a Congressman, an ambassador, or a private citizen, they would be greeted simply at the door by Lewis and then escorted into the President's office. Senator William Plumer called on Jefferson one morning and was surprised to find the President wearing "an old brown coat, red waistcoat, old corduroy small clothes, much soiled, woolen hose and slippers without heels." Plumer's description may not sound shocking to modern ears but Jefferson was wearing the 19th Century equivalent of a T-shirt, sweatpants, and house slippers. Senator Plumer actually thought Jefferson was one of the servants until he was properly introduced.

The President disliked the titles and ceremony of the European courts. Jefferson saw no reason to lavish special attention on foreign dignitaries. His deliberate inattention to diplomatic conventions nearly caused an incident when Jefferson allowed the British Ambassador to find his own seat at the dinner table. There were also lighter moments for Lewis to enjoy. When the first Turkish minister to the United States arrived for a visit he seemed unimpressed by everything except a large female slave whom he favorably compared to his "best and most expensive wife."

The President was at his best with small gatherings around the dinner table, where Lewis was almost always present. Several times a week, Jefferson would invite from two to a dozen guests to enjoy his superior collection of imported wines and the cooking of his accomplished French chef. The guests included political allies and

Many of these discussions included sensitive information. While an ambassador to France, Jefferson had learned to be cautious in his private discussions. To insure the secrecy of conversations from the domestic help, he invented a set of movable circular shelves that allowed the passage of dinner dishes between the dining room and kitchen without the presence of servants.

opponents, foreign visitors, poets, journalists, artists, and scientists. Lewis had the opportunity to discuss politics and philosophy with James Madison and Thomas Paine. On the 4th of July, 1801, he would have discussed Indian affairs with five Cherokee chiefs. Of course, Lewis' most valuable mentor was Jefferson himself who was capable of knowledgeably discussing politics, science, art, geography, or practically any other topic.

As President Kennedy recognized, Jefferson was possibly the most intelligent man to ever occupy the Oval office, but he didn't dine alone—he dined with Meriwether Lewis. The effect on Lewis was readily apparent. His writing improved. His scientific knowledge and curiosity blossomed. To be taken into the inner circle of Jefferson's presidency and Jefferson's intellect was intoxicating. Lewis began to understand and share Jefferson's vision of an American nation spanning the continent.

Jefferson's informality had to be to the liking of a frontiersman like Lewis, as did the opportunity to further his own education. Lewis prized learning. In his letters to his mother, he consistently urged her to see to the education of his younger half-brothers. Sharing the President's House placed Lewis in the perfect position for a man interested in leading an expedition across the continent. This happy coincidence and Jefferson's reference to Lewis' "knolege of the Western country" in his invitation to serve as secretary has lead many historians to conclude that Jefferson deliberately chose Lewis so he could prepare him for that mission. We will never know for sure but a larger motive may have been Lewis' knowledge of the Army officers in the western country. During the election of 1800, Jefferson had vowed to reduce the size of the army. He would need to have some criteria to evaluate which officers to dismiss and which to retain. Lewis had spent the last few years, visiting officers throughout the Ohio territory and was familiar with their politics and their competency. He compiled an exhaustive list for Jefferson detailing this information so that he could make informed decisions.

The impetus to send Lewis on the expedition most likely came near the end of 1801, with the publication of Englishman Alexander Mackenzie's book, *Voyages from Montreal, on the River St. Lawrence, Through the Continent of North America, to the Frozen and Pacific Ocean.* Mackenzie was clearly not skilled in devising catchy book titles, but he was a formidable explorer. His book describes his journey across the Canadian Rockies to the Pacific Ocean. Mackenzie knew his route was impractical for com-merce but he believed that a better route existed and that once the proper course was found "the entire command of the fur trade of North America might be obtained." He had hoped to stir the British to action. Instead, he had re-kindled Jefferson's desire to establish an American empire.

When the journals of Lewis and Clark were finally printed in 1814, they were published under a title that almost makes Mackenzie's book seem succinct: *History of the Expedition under the Command of Captains Lewis and Clark, to the Sources of the Missouri, thence Across the Rocky Mountains and down the River Columbia to the Pacific Ocean, Performed during the Years 1804-05-06.*

Jefferson ordered the book in 1801, and finally received it half a year later during his summer vacation at Monticello in 1802. Lewis was staying nearby, and they both immersed themselves in Mackenzie's book. Jefferson reasoned that since Mackenzie had found a one-day low portage across the Canadian Rockies, a similar pass must exist in the lower reaches of the mountain range. Once that pass was exploited to connect the Missouri and Columbia, the United States would be the natural beneficiary of the transcontinental commerce. As the two men read *Voyages* at Monticello, and contemplated the challenges and rewards of a journey across the Rockies, the decision to attempt the voyage must have seemed a foregone conclusion.

The exact date that Jefferson reached that conclusion is unknown, but it was around this time that he formulated the idea to send Lewis to the Pacific Ocean. Or perhaps Lewis volunteered to lead the expedition. He had already volunteered once, when he was still a teenager. We do know that beginning in the fall of 1802, Jefferson started Lewis on a crash course in the disciplines he would need to lead the expedition. Lewis drew up a budget for the journey, and Jefferson started the process of selling the expedition to Congress. In January of 1803, Congress approved the expenditure of $2,500.00 to send an officer and a dozen men on an expedition to "the Western ocean." The appropriation was well hidden inside a bill regarding Indian relations in order to avoid controversy. Congress was in an uncharacteristically generous mood that month. Just the previous week they had authorized over $9 million in the hope of buying the city of New Orleans from the French. The two expenditures, at the time unrelated, were about to combine to change the destiny of the United States.

Chapter 4

Virginia Plantation Farming

"Our governments will remain virtuous for many centuries as long as they are chiefly agricultural; and this will be as long as there shall be vacant lands in any part of America."

--Thomas Jefferson, in a letter to James Madison

According to Karl Marx, all human actions can be traced back to economic motivations. For a Virginia planter like Thomas Jefferson, George Washington, or Meriwether Lewis, the acquisition of more and more land was a fundamental motivating force. Without hundreds--if not thousands--of acres to exploit, a tobacco farmer would be bankrupt within a few years. The westward expansion of the southern colonies was a clear manifestation of this economic reality.

Tobacco wears out the soil quickly. After only three years of tobacco production, the fields were planted with wheat for a season, and then abandoned. The planter then moved his slaves to virgin land and repeated the cycle. This was an

25

Monticello, Jefferson's plantation home was not far from Meriwether Lewis' plantation home, Locust Hill. Photo from the Library of Congress, Prints and Photographs Division, LC-USZ-62-126974.

incredibly inefficient method. The system worked because it utilized the two commodities that were temporarily abundant in the colonies: land and slaves. Jefferson understood that Southern agriculture was based on a flawed foundation and worked as a botanist to develop alternatives to tobacco. He experimented with almost seventy different types of crops-- some imported from Europe, many native to America. One of Jefferson's goals for the Lewis and Clark expedition was to find new plants from the west that could be grown on eastern farms.

The drive to amass additional cropland nearly cost the colonies their independence. When the British invaded the Carolinas, Virginia Governor Thomas Jefferson was unable to lend substantial help because Virginia's resources and men were committed to helping General George Rogers Clark secure much less strategic British holdings in the West. Another effect was that "wealthy" plantation owners were perpetually in debt because of land speculation. This was a problem that was to haunt Lewis his entire life. Nearly his entire prepaid salary for the expedition went to paying off delinquent debts and buying new land.

The greater curse of plantation farming was slavery. The basis of the entire Southern economy rested squarely on the bare and beaten backs of the slaves. Jefferson knew slavery was a Faustian bargain, but he hoped that the next generation of Virginians—men like Lewis and Clark—might find a way to end the practice. Given Jefferson's critical contributions to founding our country, there is a temptation to overlook his slave-owner status as merely an unfortunate result of the time in which he lived. That is too generous an interpretation. There may have been some masters who were deluded enough to think that slaves were less than human, and that slavery was a necessary and beneficial institution to both parties; but no one with Jefferson's intelligence could possibly have believed that. He knew it was an evil practice. In his Notes on the State of Virginia, he wrote, "The whole commerce between master and slave is a perpetual exercise of the most boisterous passions, the most unremitting despotism

Lewis and Clark never had any grand ambitions about abolishing slavery but Jefferson did plant one seed that flowered. His grandson, Thomas Jefferson Randolph, proposed legislation in the Virginia Assembly that would have freed slaves born after a certain date. The plan also would have made provisions for the re-settling of all blacks outside of Virginia. His proposal went nowhere. The invention of the cotton gin reinvigorated the necessity of slaves in the plantation economy and, as a result, the attitudes of Southern planters hardened. One was quoted as saying that, "the slaves are as happy a laboring class as exists on the habitable globe."

27

This daguerreotype, taken about 1845, pictures of one of Thomas Jefferson's slaves named Lucy. She was born at Monticello and later leased to Thomas Jefferson's grandson, Thomas Jefferson Randolph. Lucy was sold at a public auction in 1827. Courtesy of the Mason County Museum, all rights reserved.

on the one part, and degrading submissions on the other. Our children see this, and learn to imitate it. The man must be a prodigy who can retain his manners and morals undepraved by such circumstances." How could Jefferson have possibly expected men like Lewis and Clark, who had grown up in such depraved circumstances, to lead the abolition of slavery?

On this issue, Jefferson had a chance to be a hero. He was the patriot who wrote, "All men are created equal." He had the rare opportunity to prove that he was more than just a great writer and formulator of ideas. The country desperately needed a man with moral courage and intellectual power to lead the abolition of slavery. Jefferson could have raised his voice and his pen in that cause. He could have taught his protégés to carry on the fight. He could have freed his own slaves as an example. Perhaps not even a man of Jefferson's stature could have engineered a peaceful resolution to the intractable problem of slavery; but a man of moral courage could have and should have made the effort. He never did. Like all human beings, Jefferson was a mixture of good and bad actions. He was a man with tremendous abilities who made invaluable contributions to our country. Unfortunately, within his impressive intellect was nestled a tragic flaw. That flaw festered in the national consciousness for almost a century before a Civil War finally resolved the crisis that Jefferson lacked the will to face.

Chapter 5

Meriwether Lewis

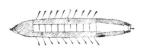

"Captain Lewis is brave, prudent, habituated to the woods, & familiar with Indian manners & character. He is not regularly educated, but he possesses a great mass of accurate observation on all the subjects of nature which present themselves here, & will therefore readily select those only in his new route which shall be new."

> --Thomas Jefferson, in a letter to Dr. Benjamin Rush, explaining his decision to make Lewis the leader of the transcontinental expedition

If Jefferson did not deliberately choose Lewis as his secretary in order to prepare him for the expedition, then it was an incredible feat of serendipity. Lewis was the ideal candidate. He was always in search of adventure. He was a skilled outdoorsman. He had a rudimentary understanding of the necessary science and was willing and able to learn the rest. He was loyal to Jefferson. He was brave, some would say to a fault. He was a natural leader of men, though he never

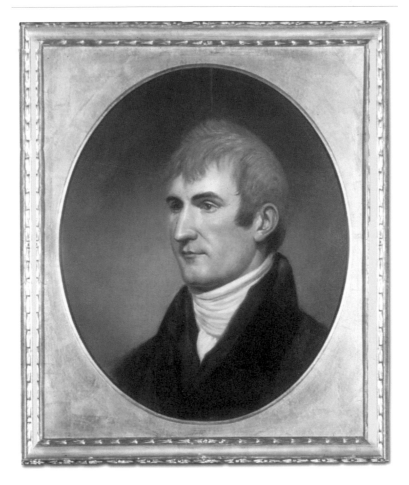

Meriwether Lewis by Charles Willson Peale, from life, 1807
Independence National Historical Park

had much luck with women.

Lewis was born in Albemarle County, Virginia in 1774, not far from Jefferson's estate at Monticello. War broke out with England the following year, and Meriwether's father, William, enlisted at his own expense. When Meriwether was five, his father joined the family for a brief visit at

31

Cloverfields, his mother Lucy's childhood home. On November 12, 1779, William said good-bye to his family and headed back to the Revolutionary War. He didn't get far. The Rivanna River was flooding, but William attempted to cross anyway. His horse was swept away in midstream and drowned. Somehow, William struggled to shore, then made the cold and wet journey back to the Cloverfields on foot. He died of pneumonia two days later.

The common practice in Virginia was for widows to remarry quickly. Thus, Meriwether acquired a stepfather just six months later when his mother married William Marks. Within a few years, the Marks family moved from Virginia to settle a new colony in northeastern Georgia. Here, Lewis had his first encounter with angry Indians. The badly outnumbered settlers had gathered in the woods to hide from Indians after a cabin had been attacked. Hungry and cold, one settler foolishly lit a fire. The smoke and light were signs sure to be seen by any nearby Indians. The settlers would be easy prey once they were discovered in the open forest. Before long, a rifle shot was heard. The settlers knew they were in trouble. The men rushed for their guns. The women gathered the children. Only one person—10-year-old Meriwether Lewis—had the composure to remember the fire. He quickly doused it and likely saved many lives.

There is another anecdote about his poise under pressure. At about the same age he was crossing a field with some friends. To their surprise, a startled bull charged the party of young boys. Meriwether raised his gun, took careful aim, and shot the bull dead. Twenty years later, he would not be so fortunate with a grizzly bear.

At age thirteen, he decided to return to Albemarle County. He needed an education, something he could not acquire in the backwoods of Georgia. Soon, he would assume responsibility for his father's plantation. This must have been both an exciting and daunting prospect for young

Meriwether. He would be responsible for almost 2,000 acres of land and two dozen slaves. Although he did not know it at the time, he would also become responsible for his mother and younger siblings with William Marks' death in 1791. Procuring an education was no simple achievement for Meriwether. Public schools did not exist. Young boys were educated in the boarding houses of clergymen. Meriwether had a difficult time finding a teacher that was both available and competent. For years, he shuffled between several teachers, some worse than others. In a letter to his brother Reuben, he wrote that his elders had decided that he had "got well acquanted with the English Grammer, and mite learn Geogrphy at Home. Upon this, I concluded to stay at Uncle Peacy Gilmers, and go to School to a Master in the Neighbourhood, . . . in Order to get acquanted with Figurs, where I am now Stationed . . . . I should like very much to have some of your Sport, fishing, and hunting, provided I could be doing Something, that will no Doubt be more to my advantag herafter." Had some of his "elders" seen this letter they might have changed their minds about the completeness of his education. In 1792, after less than five years of schooling, Meriwether returned to Georgia where he supervised the move of his newly widowed mother and his brothers and sisters back to Albemarle County. They returned to his father's plantation, called Locust Hill. His formal education was over. Lewis was ready to assume his place as a Virginia planter.

Fifty years later and several hundred miles to the north, Henry David Thoreau, watched a farmer toiling behind his plowhorse, and lamented the loss of freedom that was the unintended side effect of such responsibility.

"I see young men, my townsmen, whose misfortune it is to have inherited farms, houses, barns, cattle, and farming tools; for these are more easily acquired than got rid of. Better if they had been born in the open pasture and suckled by a wolf, that they might have seen with clearer eyes what field they were called to labor in."

Meriwether Lewis would have read that passage and shouted, "Amen!" He was not called to be a farmer. Most teenagers would have reveled in the aristocratic life of the Virginia planter. Not Meriwether Lewis. He longed not for wealth and security but for adventure. He lasted only two years running Locust Hill. After that he would seldom live in one place more than a few months. In 1793, he hoped to escape from the plantation by joining the Michaux expedition. When that failed he chose the path traveled by so many other young boys seeking adventure: he enlisted in the Army.

It was hardly the adventure Lewis had anticipated. He signed up to "support the glorious cause of Liberty, and my country." What he got was a long march through rain and mud to track down the few remaining leaders of the Whisky Rebellion, who quickly fled to Louisiana. When his militia was sent home and Lewis was faced with the prospect of returning to Locust Hill, he volunteered to stay with a small occupying force in Western Pennsylvania. When that service was over, he enlisted in the regular army. In a letter home, his sensible advice to his younger brother likely hides an ulterior motive:

"I wish Rubin to amuse himself with ucefull books. If he will pay attention he may be adequate to the task (of running Locust Hill) the ensuing year." He wanted Rueben to be able to run the plantation so he wouldn't be forced to come home and do it himself.

Lewis' career in the Army very nearly came to a quick end because of his politics and drinking. He was a Republican in a sea of Federalist officers, a distinction that would later qualify him to be Jefferson's secretary. In 1795, it was a decided disadvantage. One night, he got drunk and argued politics with a Lieutenant Eliott. Eliott threw Lewis out of his own. Lewis responded, as any self-respecting Southern gentlemen would, with an invitation to duel. Dueling was expressly forbidden by Army regulations, and Eliott brought charges. Lewis was court-martialed on November 6, 1795. He plead not guilty, though he undoubtedly was. Fortunately for Lewis, his commanding officer, General Anthony Wayne, disagreed with the prohibition on dueling. He considered dueling a quick and inexpensive alternative to court-martials. Thus, Lewis was acquitted and the General used the occasion to make plain his policy that future court-martials for dueling would be unnecessary.

Ensign Lewis was promptly transferred to the Chosen Rifle Company to separate him from Eliott. His new captain was his future co-commander on the expedition, William Clark. They only served together for six months, yet during that time they developed a mutual friendship and respect that later made them willing to travel together into the unknown. For the next four years, Lewis served in various positions throughout the Old Northwest (modern Ohio, Indiana, and Michigan). He was eventually promoted to captain and spent two years traveling the length of the Ohio River as a paymaster. Many men would have been lonely wandering up and down the sparsely populated Ohio country. Lewis thrived. Ever since he was a boy, he had enjoyed being in the woods alone. Later, on the expedition, he preferred to leave Clark on the boat and explore the river valleys with a few select companions or by himself. During this time, Lewis refined many of the skills that would prove valuable during the expedition. He piloted a keelboat. He dealt with Indians. He learned to take care of himself with only a rifle and ingenuity.

Meanwhile, far away in the nation's capital, events were converging that would change Lewis' destiny. His friend and neighbor, Thomas Jefferson, narrowly defeated the incumbent President John Adams in 1801. Hours before he left office, President Adams packed the federal judiciary and the Army officer corps with Federalist appointees in order to insure a Federalist presence for years to come. The new Republican President would clearly need an ally in the military and a man with first-hand knowledge of the existing officer corps. Jefferson's invitation to be secretary reached Lewis in Pittsburgh on March 7, 1801, three days after the inauguration. On April 1, he arrived in Washington. His apprenticeship to Thomas Jefferson had begun.

Chapter 6

Preparations for the Journey

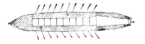

Indian Presents
  5 lbs. White Glass Beads mostly small
  12 Red Silk Handkerchiefs
  144 Small cheap looking Glasses
  4 Vials of Phosforus
  144 Small cheap Scizors
  2 lbs. Vermillion
  6 Belts of narrow Ribbons colours assorted
  50 lbs. Spun Tobacco
  15 Sheets of Copper Cut into strips
  18 Cheap brass Combs
  24 Blankets

—from Lewis's list of necessary supplies, June 30, 1803.

Jefferson had just presented Lewis with the opportunity of a lifetime: the chance to explore an unknown continent at government expense and become a national hero in the process. At the beginning of 1803, they decided on a timetable for expedition. Lewis would descend the Ohio to the Mississippi that summer and proceed as far up the river as possible before winter forced them to camp. In 1804, Lewis would finish the trip to the Pacific, make the return voyage, and be back in Washington reporting to Jefferson sometime during the winter of 1804-05. That left him only the first few months of 1803 to make all necessary plans, procure all of the supplies, and finish his crash course in astronomy, botany zoology, and medicine.

The first order of business was a trip to the Army's arsenal at Harper's Ferry, where Lewis ordered guns, knives, tomahawks, and fishhooks. The anticipated one-week stay stretched out to a month because Lewis insisted on personally supervising the construction of a collapsible boat he cautiously christened, Experiment; a name unlikely to inspire much confidence in his men. Lewis planned to haul the boat to the Great Falls of the Missouri, portage it across, then assemble it on the other side. This would allow the men to continue the journey via water instead of on foot or horseback. Lewis was thrilled with the final product, which weighed only 44 pounds and could carry nearly a ton when fully assembled. Jefferson's infatuation with inventing had clearly rubbed off on Lewis.

Lewis had another clever idea. He had the quartermaster at Harper's Ferry put the gunpowder into lead canisters. Once empty, these lead canisters could be melted down into balls. Each canister provided exactly enough powder to shoot the balls from which it was composed.

He also bought almost 200 pounds of dried soup, one of his largest single expenditures. As it turned out, the men hated the soup, and it was consumed only when the alternative was starvation. Even then, it was a difficult decision.

By mid-April, Lewis was in Lancaster, Pennsylvania learning astronomy from Andrew Ellicott. Ellicott also taught Lewis to use a sextant so that he could make measurements regarding latitude and longitude. He studied for almost three weeks then pushed on to Philadelphia. There he continued his astronomical studies, and added training in medicine, botany, and even paleontology with the leading faculty at the University of Pennsylvania.

Lewis also continued his shopping. He found ink and pencils for the journals, oilskin bags for storing documents, tents, candles, clothes, and tobacco. He purchased trading goods for the Indians: various colors of glass beads, scissors, thread, silk, knives, and combs. Lewis knew he would soon be beyond any supply posts. Once past St. Louis there would be no opportunity to purchase supplies from any white man. A simple mistake buying supplies in Philadelphia could doom the expedition before it ever began.

In hindsight, Lewis was a prudent planner. He ran out of a few important items like whisky, tobacco, and salt. These shortages were inconvenient but not fatal. He was careful to have plenty of the three items that were absolutely indispensable: guns, powder, and ammunition. In fact, when the men floated into St. Louis nearly two years after they left, there were enough of those items to repeat the journey.

With his training completed and most of his supplies ready, Lewis was ready to return to Washington. He wanted to have a final meeting with Jefferson to discuss his orders. He also planned to propose William Clark's name as a co-commander for the expedition. After that, Lewis would turn his course west until he reached the ocean.

Chapter 7

Doctor Lewis

"I have formerly said that there is but one fever in the world. Be not startled, Gentlemen, follow me and I will say that there is but one disease in the world. The proximate cause of the disease is irregular convulsive action in the vascular system affected."

--Dr. Benjamin Rush, Lewis' chief medical advisor, promoting his theory that all disease is caused by problems related to blood circulation.

Lewis vacillated about including a doctor in the expedition. At first, he planned to bring one. At Philadelphia, he changed his mind and studied medicine himself with Dr. Benjamin Rush. Later at Wheeling, Virginia, he told Dr. William Patterson that he could join the expedition. Sadly for Patterson, he was late reaching the boat and Lewis left without him. Partly by choice and partly by default, Lewis became responsible for the health of his men.

Rush's instruction primarily consisted of two treatments that he considered appropriate for just about any malady. The

Dr. Benjamin Rush, medical advisor to Meriwether Lewis. Painting from the Library of Congress, Prints and Photographs Division, LC-USZ-62-097104.

first was bloodletting. Rush reasoned that sickness was caused by the injurious effects of some agent within the patient's body. The logical solution then was to remove that harmful element. In the late 18th Century, this was medical orthodoxy. During the final hours of his illness, the physicians attending George Washington drained nearly half the blood in his body. Lewis followed Rush's counsel and bled his patients regularly.

The second treatment was the liberal use of his patented "Dr. Rush's Pills." The pills were mostly mercury with a little chlorine and jalap. Their efficacy as medicine is debatable. What is certain is that they were a laxative of tremendous power; thus the common nickname, "Thunder Clappers." Lewis took 50 dozen on the trip. One of the illnesses that could actually be treated with Thunder Clappers was venereal disease. Mercury was a common treatment until the mid-20th Century. Lewis must have prescribed these pills regularly. At Fort Clatsop on the Oregon coast, he implored the men to stay away from some infected Indian women, as he did not want to dispense another round of Rush's pills. The mercury provided only a temporary cure. Symptoms often re-appeared, and were again treated with Thunder Clappers. Some historians have suggested that these large doses of mercury may have contributed to the early deaths that were prevalent among the Corps of Discovery.

In 2002, archaeologists claimed to have found a Lewis and Clark campsite near Lolo, Montana. The archaeologists knew they had the right spot when they found a rectangular depression they surmised was the latrine. Soil analysis of the latrine area showed mercury concentrations many times higher than the nearby soil—a sure sign that Dr. Lewis had been there.

Equally useful to Lewis was the training in herb therapy he received from his mother. While Lewis was scouting ahead in search of the Great Falls, he was incapacitated with a violent case of dysentery. He healed himself the same evening with a chokecherry decoction.

A few days later, after finding the Great Falls, Lewis returned to camp to find Sacajawea nearly dead. This was a serious problem. The expedition could not afford to lose their Shoshone interpreter just as her services would become most critical. Her pulse was weak and irregular. Her fingers

Rush sent Lewis with a list of suggestions on maintaining good health among the men. These included wearing flannel next to the skin and resting in a horizontal position. Library of Congress, Manuscript Division.

and arms were twitching. Clark had tried bleeding her as well as a poultice of bark and opium. Lewis continued this treatment and also had her drink the water from a nearby sulfur spring. This seemed to improve her condition.

Three days later, Sacajawea's condition became serious again. Lewis had asked Sacajawea's husband, Toussaint Charboneau, to supervise his wife's diet and included specific instructions regarding approved and forbidden foods. In total disregard, Charboneau let Sacajawea gather and eat some raw roots known as "white apples" and some fish. Lewis gave her several doses of saltpeter and thirty drops of laudanum. By the morning she was feeling better. Within a few days she was well.

Lewis also learned new remedies from the Indians. When Sacajawea was struggling to give birth, the Indians suggested that she be given the powder of a crushed rattlesnake tail. Lewis did as advised, and she delivered within fifteen minutes. Even so, Lewis was skeptical of the potion's efficacy but considered it "worthy of future experiments."

The expedition's medical knowledge provided benefits in another way. When they had virtually no trading goods but desperately needed supplies from the Nez Perce to get back across the Rockies, Clark put out his shingle and acted as doctor. By a fortunate coincidence, Clark had given some simple treatment to a Nez Perce warrior with a sore leg the previous year. Luckily, the treatment had worked and Clark was regarded as a great medicine man. He treated up to 50 patients a day of such ailments as rheumatism, ulcers, and infections. Payment was typically a dog, which the men ate immediately. Sometimes, Clark was able to help his patients, but he had no illusions about his medical skills. His main concern was not to harm anyone, and if a few benefited from his treatment, so much the better.

One of his most difficult cases was a Nez Perce chief of some renown who had lost the use of his arms and legs.

Treating a chief was a delicate matter. To accidentally harm him or fail to cure him could have dire consequences. Clark had no idea what was causing the problem. There was no pain that normally accompanied rheumatism. There was no withering of the limbs that would indicate a stroke. Clark took a wild guess that the paralysis was due to some unusual combination of roots, which were common in the Nez Perce diet. He recommended a diet of fish and meat and a cold bath every day (the frontier equivalent of, "Take two aspirin and call me in the morning.") Clark also gave him some cream of tartar and flour sulfur to take every third day. At his next visit, Lewis reported that, "this poor wretch thinks that he feels himself somewhat better but to me there appears to be no alteration. We are at a loss what to do for this unfortunate man." At this point, as at so many other times, luck intervened on the expedition's behalf. William Bratton had been suffering from severe back pain. John Shields suggested a sweat bath. They dug a small hole for the procedure, and tried it on Bratton with some success. Seeing this, the Nez Perce implored Lewis to try the sweat bath on their chief. They enlarged the hole to allow the man's father to hold him during the process, and accommodated the request. Afterwards, the chief complained of great pain, and Lewis gave him some laudanum to help him rest that night. Lewis and Clark must have spent a restless night wondering if they had permanently injured a Nez Perce chief. Miraculously, the next day, the chief could move his hands and arms. He asked to have the treatments repeated. After a few more days, he could use his legs. Lewis reported that, "I begin to entertain strong hope of his restoration by these sweats." If pressed for a medical explanation, Lewis could have offered no scientific reasoning for the chief's recovery but the facts remained. A Nez Perce chief had recovered under the care of Dr. Lewis and the men of the expedition were the fortunate beneficiaries.

Chapter 8

Last Meeting with the President

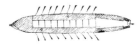

"From my ideas of Capt. Lewis he will be much more likely, in case of difficulty, to push too far, than to recede too soon. Would it not be well to change the term, 'certain destruction' into 'probable destruction' & to add—that these dangers are never to be encountered, which vigilance precaution & attention can secure against, at a reasonable expense."

> --Attorney General Levi Lincoln, in a letter to Jefferson suggesting that they change Lewis' instructions so that he would be less likely to pick a fight with the Indians

The relationship between Jefferson and Lewis was almost like father and son. Lewis had never known his real father. He had been forced to grow up quickly with occasional oversight from his stepfather and uncles. Jefferson had taken a genuine interest in him. From the way Lewis describes Jefferson in the journals, his admiration is obvious. They had spent two years as the only occupants of the President's House. During this time, Jefferson trained Lewis in science, politics, and the habits of a Virginia gentleman. Now, Lewis was about to undertake a feat that, if successful, would make his new father honored and proud.

The relationship was not all one-sided. Lewis filled an immense void for the President. Jefferson's family life was painfully tragic. In the nine years between 1775 and 1784, he lost his mother, his wife at age 33, and four of his six children. While Lewis was in St. Louis in 1804, Jefferson lost one of his two remaining daughters. Lewis was more than a secretary; he was a protégé, an advisor, and a confidant, almost a surrogate son. With the possible exception of James Madison, no one in Washington knew more about Thomas Jefferson and his government than Lewis. Now, Jefferson was sending this brave son off on a dangerous mission. The risks were great. The rewards would also be great.

In June of 1803, Jefferson and Lewis had a final chance to discuss the expedition. The President also presented Lewis with his formal written instructions as the commanding officer. The primary objective of the expedition was to find a water route across the continent, but that was just the beginning of Jefferson's grand purposes.

Lewis was also instructed to establish friendly relations with the Indians in order to set the stage for a vast American fur trade. Jefferson had a very practical attitude toward the Indians. He knew that the population of the United States would inevitably move west. The Indians might resist but they could never triumph. Jefferson hoped that the Indians could be fully assimilated into the United States. Towards this end, he

He held no such hopes for the integration of Negro slaves.

instructed Lewis to ask the Indian chiefs he encountered to come to Washington and see the culture and technology of their "Great Father." He also told him to extend an invitation to the Indians to have their children raised and educated in the states. Jefferson must have been aware of the most serious problem facing Indians in 1803: smallpox. Many of the tribes Lewis and Clark were to visit had already lost up to 80% of their population to this disease. Lewis was to take an experimental vaccine to the Indians and instruct them in its use.

There was also the question of what to do in case of an Indian attack. Jefferson knew the Americans would be seen as economic competitors by some of the British-aligned tribes along the Missouri. He had no idea what to expect from Indians west of the Mandan villages. Encounters with hostile Indians were almost inevitable. Here, Jefferson had to strike a delicate balance. Of course, he wanted the party to reach the Pacific but he also wanted no casualties in achieving that goal, neither among the party nor the Indians. Ultimately, the decision would be made by Lewis but Jefferson instructed, "To your own discretion, therefore, must be left the degree of danger you may risk, and the point at which you should decline, only saying, we wish you to err on the side of your safety, and to bring back your party safe, even if it be with less information."

Lewis also had many scientific duties. He was to catalog new species of plant and animal life, search for fossils, map the locations of volcanoes, and list the types of minerals encountered. Jefferson wanted charts showing data on the climates of each region encountered. He also wanted to know how the climate affected the plant and animal life. When did the plants flower? When did the leaves fall? When did the animals migrate or hibernate? Jefferson was a scientist with many questions.

Finally, Jefferson told Lewis to find a ship when he reached the Pacific and send his notes home along with two men. If Lewis considered the return voyage too dangerous by land he was to take the entire party home by ship. Naturally, Lewis would have no money to buy such a passage. To remedy this, Jefferson gave him a virtually unlimited letter of credit, which allowed him to draw on the funds of any branch of the U.S. government anywhere in the world for any amount of money.

Given the scope of Jefferson's instructions, one issue became apparent quickly: the need for a second officer. Almost immediately, Lewis thought of William Clark. They had served together only briefly yet they had quickly formed favorable opinions of one another. Their mutual respect, trust, and friendship are readily apparent in the letters they exchanged in preparation for the journey.

On June 19th, 1803, Lewis invited Clark to join the expedition: "Thus my friend you have a summary view of the plan, the means and the objects of this expedition. If therefore there is anything under those circumstances, in this enterprise, which would induce you to participate with me in it's fatiegues, it's dangers and it's honors, believe me there is no man on earth with whom I should feel equal pleasure in sharing them as with yourself."

The mail moved so slowly that it was over a month before Lewis received Clark's emphatic response: "This is an undertaking fraited with many dificulties, but My friend I do assure you that no man lives with whome I would perfur to undertake Such a Trip &c. as yourself."

Lewis' respect for Clark was so great that he offered him a co-command—a concept anathema in almost any military situation. Yet over the course of the journey the commanders agreed on almost every topic except the palatability of dog meat. (Clark never could get used to it.)

Their co-command was not redundant. Lewis was fascinated with the scientific aspects of the mission. He was content to wander the new territory gathering specimens and making observations. Clark was a better waterman and mapmaker, and better at handling the day-to-day supervision of the men. Clark was more even-tempered than Lewis, who was subject to fits of melancholy and anger. Lewis was a better writer and, sad to say, a better speller. Although this was never expressly spoken, co-command also eliminated a leadership crisis if one of the captains was killed. Whether it was incredible insightfulness or just good luck, Lewis picked a man who exactly complemented his own strengths and weaknesses.

Once Lewis had his final instructions and co-commander in place, he had only one last bit of unfinished business in Washington D.C. He needed to write to his mom. No doubt, all sons setting off on dangerous adventures have the impulse to set their mothers' minds at ease. However, Lewis' letter may stand alone in terms of spouting the most bold-faced lies any mother was ever expected to believe. Mrs. Lewis' son was about to set off on a journey never successfully completed by any explorer, through unknown territory and hostile Indians, with unsure food supplies and untried transportation. This is how he described it to her: "The nature of this expedition is by no means dangerous, my rout will be altogether thorugh tribes of Indians who are perfectly friendly to the United States, therefore consider the chances of life just as much in my favor on this trip as I should conceive them were I to remain at home."

He would certainly have more exciting tales to tell when he returned to her over three years later.

Chapter 9

The Louisiana Purchase

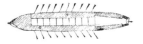

"A great waste, a wilderness unpeopled with any beings except wolves and wandering Indians."

--Article in the Federalist Boston newspaper, Columbian Centinel,
describing the land Jefferson had just purchased from Napoleon

Lewis had a final bit of good news before he left Washington. He would not be exploring exclusively foreign territory. He would not need to deceive the French or Spanish about his true intentions—at least not completely. In fact, throughout most of the journey he would be traveling on U.S. soil.

All of this came about because of a Haitian slave named Toussaint L'ouverture. France had acquired the rights to all territory drained by the Mississippi River when Rene' de La Salle explored the Mississippi back in 1682. Of course, La Salle had no idea what he was claiming, but the claim stuck—legally, if not practically. In 1762, France ceded the territory to Spain. Forty years later, in 1802, by secret treaty, Louisiana

51

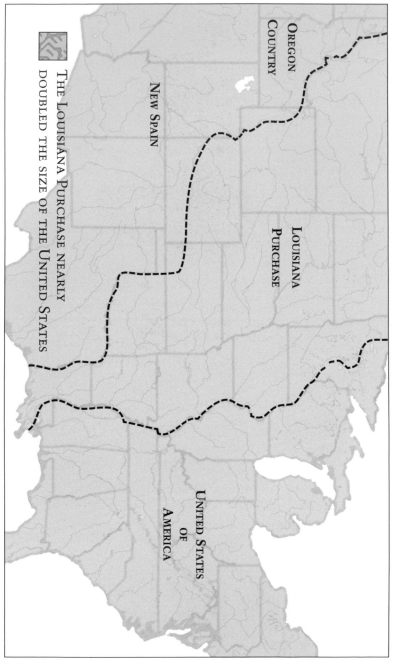

THE LOUISIANA PURCHASE NEARLY
DOUBLED THE SIZE OF THE UNITED STATES

OREGON
COUNTRY

NEW SPAIN

LOUISIANA
PURCHASE

UNITED STATES
OF
AMERICA

Toussaint L'Overture was largely responsible for Haitian independence. The disastrous French offensive in Haiti convinced Napoleon to sell Louisiana. Painting from the Library of Congress, Prints and Photographs Division, LC-USZ-62-7862.

was returned to France. Napoleon's grand scheme was to use Louisiana to supply his New World capital in Hispaniola (modern Haiti). There was one major problem with Napoleon's plan. Although he had the title to Hispaniola and Louisiana, he had no control over either territory. Without immediate, decisive action, the Americans and British would soon overrun Louisiana; and Hispaniola, though technically a French colony, was governed by a former slave, and now a French General, Toussaint L'ouverture,

L'ouverture had earned this position by successfully leading the slaves against each of the great powers of Europe. During the 1790's, he successfully fought the French, the Spanish, and the British. Napoleon himself had recognized L'ouverture as the legitimate leader of Hispaniola. However, Napoleon was nothing if not ambitious. Why not have both a New World and Old World Empire? France would then rival, if not surpass, England as a world power. When he was able to re-acquire Louisiana, he decided to re-acquire Hispaniola as well. Napoleon sent an army of 35,000 troops and 80 warships, lead by his brother-in-law, to conquer the small island. What should have been an easy victory turned into a disaster. Half his troops were dead of yellow fever within a year. L'ouverture's army fought fiercely. Napoleon was forced to withdraw, and Haiti became the first independent black nation in the New World.

Incidentally, this free black nation so close to the United States terrified Jefferson and his slave-owning neighbors. In 1805-6, he suspended all trade with Haiti. The economic impact of this embargo was a decisive factor in the failure of the new government, which Jefferson blamed on the inability of blacks to govern themselves.

The defeat in Hispaniola rendered Louisiana practically worthless to Napoleon. The only question left was how to dispose of it on the most favorable terms. Besides, Napoleon no had no more money or troops to spare on a French New World Empire, especially if he wanted to control Europe, which he most certainly did. The simplest and best solution was to sell the territory to the United States. At the same time he would be keeping Louisiana out of British hands and creating a new power to rival Britain that "sooner or later, will someday humble her pride."

Napoleon's minister made the offer and the Americans jumped at the opportunity. Not waiting to see if the transaction was financially possible or Constitutionally legal

(Jefferson was quite sure the purchase was unconstitutional, but proceeded anyway), Jefferson's negotiators quickly agreed to the deal. Congress went along.

Not since the legendary purchase of Manhattan Island for $24 worth of beads had there been such a one-sided real estate transaction. Napoleon knew the Louisiana Purchase was a bargain for the United States. He was simply making the best of a bad situation. Jefferson and his negotiators in France could hardly believe their good fortune. With the stroke of a pen they had doubled the size of the country. They had secured control of the Mississippi River, which was imperative to the commerce of every state west of the Appalachians. Had Napoleon decided instead to pursue a French empire in North America, he would never have prevailed but the resulting chaos could have easily lead to decades of armed conflict between the U.S., France, Spain, Britain, possibly even Russia, and of course, the Indians. Only a few of Jefferson's most vehement Federalist opponents questioned the clear wisdom of the purchase, calling the new territory a wasteland and a "great curse." Part of the benefit of the Lewis and Clark expedition would be some concrete proof of the commercial value of the new land.

Jefferson wrote Lewis the day after the treaty was received to tell him the news. Now, Lewis would be exploring U.S. territory and informing the Indians that Jefferson was their new "Great Father."

Chapter 10

Lewis Heads West

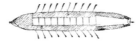

"... being invited on by some of the gentlemen present to try my airgun which I had purchased brought it on shore charged it and fired myself seven times fifty five yards with pretty good success; after which a Mr. Blaze Cenas being unacquainted with the management of the gun suffered her to discharge herself accidentaly the ball passed through the hat of a woman about 40 yards distanc cutting her temple about the fourth of the diameter of the ball; shee feel instantly and the blood gusing from her temple we were all in the greatest consternation supposed she was dead ... "

--August 30, 1803, Meriwether Lewis, on the very first day
of the expedition

The day after Independence Day, 1803, Lewis set out for Pittsburgh. He had already sent the supplies he had procured at Harper's Ferry and Philadelphia ahead by wagon. He had also arranged for the construction of a 55-foot keelboat by a Pittsburgh boat-builder. If all went well, he would meet his supplies, load the boat, pick up a few men and be on his way by July 20th.

Nothing went well. The driver who was carrying the supplies from Harper's Ferry had left the guns and iron-framed boat behind. They were too heavy for his team. Lewis immediately contracted with another driver to bring the items. This driver also "disappointed" Lewis and had to be replaced.

When Lewis arrived in Pittsburgh on July 15th, he found the Ohio River rapidly descending and his keelboat nowhere near completion. The contract called for completion by the 20th. This date was clearly not going to be met. Lewis explained the urgency of the task to the contractor who promised to be done by July 30th. July 30th came and still the boat was not even half-done. Lewis was furious. He would have gladly fired the man but no one else in Pittsburgh was qualified to finish the job. He had no choice but to nag and threaten. He supervised much of the work personally. To make matters worse, the boat-builder was drunk much of the time. He missed work often and argued with his workmen. As Lewis waited helplessly and watched the water sink every day, he must have calculated where his expedition should be and where it would not be by the time the Missouri froze. He was not a man who controlled his temper easily. He had nearly fought a duel with a fellow officer just a few years before. His temper would flare up again several times during the voyage. It must have taken every ounce of his self-control to keep from beating this man who threatened to cost him an entire year of the mission. Perhaps to give himself a distraction, Lewis spent twenty dollars to buy a Newfoundland dog he named "Seaman."

The boat was finally ready on August 31st. Lewis noted that "those who pretend to be acquainted with the navigation of the river declare it impracticable to descend it." Lewis left anyway—three hours after the boat was finished.

A sketch of the keelboat made by William Clark. Courtesy of the Yale Collection of Americana, Beinecke Rare Book and Manuscript Library.

A mere three miles downstream, the expedition nearly suffered its first fatality. Lewis stopped at a small settlement and was showing off an air gun he had purchased in Philadelphia. This gun was powered by pumping the stock full of air. When fully pressured, the gun was nearly as effective as a typical rifle. It was also quiet, making it a favorite for poachers. The locals were fascinated. Lewis shot the gun a few times and then passed it around for everyone to see. It is hard to imagine that Lewis pumped up a loaded gun and then handed it to the pioneers for inspection yet that is exactly what he did. Inevitably, the gun went off. A woman screamed and blood gushed from the side of her head. Lewis must have felt like the unluckiest man alive. Barely half a day into the expedition, he was already over a month behind schedule, and now he was an accessory to manslaughter. Frantically, he rushed over to the woman. On closer inspection, they discovered that the bullet had merely grazed her. The wound was bloody but definitely non-fatal. Lewis learned his lesson. He showed the gun many more times—to the Indians and others—but never when it was pressured and loaded.

The voyage down the Ohio River was difficult. In places the water was only 6" deep. That first day, the men had to disembark several times to push and pull the boat across some low passages. It was backbreaking work. They made only ten miles. Lewis gave the men some whisky and went to bed early.

The next days of the voyage were no easier. Sometimes, they would have to unload the keelboat completely to force it across the low passages. Sometimes even then, the exertions of the men were insufficient. Lewis would then have to find a local farmer to pull the boat with his oxen. These delays, coupled with the high prices charged by the settlers to help, were immensely frustrating to Lewis. Seaman was able to provide some relief. Lewis enjoyed watching his new dog catch squirrels swimming across the river. He would then fry them for dinner, pronouncing them a "plesent food." Squirrel would be the first of many unique meats tasted by the expedition.

After about ten days of difficult travel, the expedition reached Wheeling, Ohio, where the river thankfully started to deepen. Lewis quickly covered the next 200 miles to Cincinnati in two weeks. Here, he stopped for a week to rest the men and to send letters to Clark and Jefferson. He updated Clark on the progress of the voyage and discussed the qualifications of the men they should take on the journey. Many sons of wealthy families had petitioned both Lewis and

Clark to be included, and both men were in agreement that such men were of no value. They needed skilled frontiersmen, hunters, and artisans. Lewis had already found two such men in John Colter and George Shannon. He had also been forced to dismiss several men and, on one occasion, found two of his men so drunk that he had them "picked up and thrown into the boat."

His letter to Jefferson probably gave the President several sleepless nights. Lewis was a wanderer. The President knew that. That was partly why he had been selected to lead the party. On October 3, he wrote to the President about his improvised plan to explore the Southwest. Lewis had already realized that his original timeline was useless. He could make no appreciable distance up the Missouri. Instead, he would split the men and take a group on horseback towards Santa Fe. Clark would take the other half to a different, unspecified "interesting portion of the country." Lewis reasoned that the additional information obtained would help Jefferson sell the value of the enterprise to his Federalist opponents. In the midst of one of the greatest adventures any American could undertake, Lewis could not stand to wait through the winter. He wanted to explore more unknown territory.

What would Jefferson have given for a cell phone at the moment he read Lewis' letter? His brave secretary was jeopardizing the search for a Northwest Passage on U.S. soil to look for heaven only knows what in the middle of hostile Spanish territory. Unlike Lewis, Jefferson realized that the expedition would have surely been captured and probably imprisoned by the Spanish had they started toward the gold mines of New Mexico. Jefferson wrote his only direct order to Lewis: "You must not undertake the winter excursion which you propose in yours of Oct. 3." He reminded him of the primary purpose of the expedition—to find the water route to the Pacific. Then Jefferson cautioned Lewis, in a firm tone, to avoid unnecessary risks. He mailed the letter

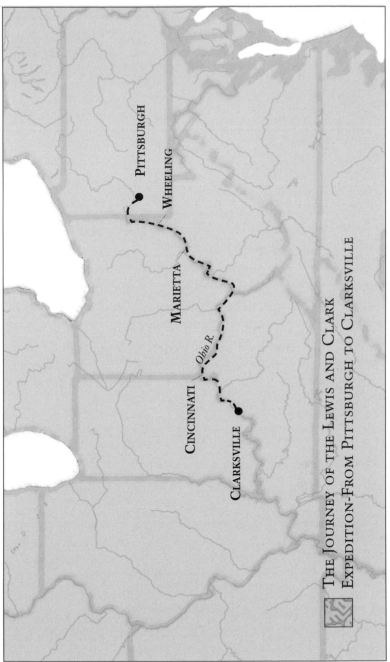

PITTSBURGH

WHEELING

MARIETTA

Ohio R.

CINCINNATI

CLARKSVILLE

THE JOURNEY OF THE LEWIS AND CLARK
EXPEDITION-FROM PITTSBURGH TO CLARKSVILLE

knowing full well it would do no good. If Lewis decided to venture off into Spanish territory, the President's countermanding order would be well behind him.

Just after sending the Letter to the President, Lewis started back down the Ohio. He covered one hundred miles in ten days, reaching the falls of the Ohio on October 14th. On opposite sides of the falls, were the cities of Louisville and Clarksville. Here awaited Lewis' friend and co-commander, William Clark.

Just a few years after Lewis and Clark returned, Zebulon Pike led another expedition to survey the new U.S. territory. He made the mistake that Lewis had only contemplated and slipped briefly into Spanish territory. His journey was thus terminated in a Spanish jail.

Chapter 11

William Clark

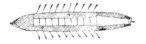

"Yr Brother, William is gone out, as a cadet, with Genl. Scott, on the Expedition. He is a youth of solid & promising parts, and as brave as Caesar."

--Letter to Jonathan Clark, May 30, 1791

The Clark family was originally from Albemarle County, Virginia, neighbors of both the Lewis's and the Jefferson's. Just before their fifth child, William, was born in 1770, the family moved to an inherited plantation closer to the coast. During the Revolutionary War, William's older brother, George Rogers Clark, successfully fought the British in the Northwest Territories. He had the poor judgment to trust the Virginia legislature's promises to reimburse him for expenses incurred during the campaign. This was a financial setback from which the family never fully recovered. In 1785, they decided to move west into the territory which had just been conquered by their oldest brother. This move brought the

63

William Clark. Co-commander of the Corps of Discovery.

"William Clark by Charles Willson Peale, from life, 1807-1808"
Independence National Historical Park

Clarks into close proximity to many hostile Indians. From this point on, the destiny of William Clark was intertwined with the Indians: first, as a soldier against them; second; as an explorer among them; and third, as a governor and advocate for their welfare.

At the end of the Revolutionary War, Congress had promptly disbanded the military, thinking never to use it again. By 1784, the entire federal army consisted of 80 men— 25 at Fort Pitt and 55 at West Point. State militias were responsible for the defense of the country. This was welcome news to the frontier Indians who were tired of being pushed farther west. They attacked the U.S. settlers without fear. Between 1783 and 1790, Indians killed over one thousand Kentucky settlers. Ohio was worse. This was the predicament the Clarks were about to encounter.

President Washington finally did send some federal troops to protect the settlers. Though only a teenager, William Clark and his brothers participated in many of these skirmishes. The Army's efforts to control the Indians ranged from ineffective to embarrassing. The culmination occurred in November of 1791. General St. Clair led a force of 4,000 men, possibly including young William Clark. Some of the soldiers' wives even tagged along. His regiment faced the typical problems-- meager supplies, inadequate training, and poor discipline. The final blow came when the whisky ran out. Sixty men deserted and were chased down. Tecumseh and his band of Shawnee scouts observed the chaos and recommended a sudden attack on the troops. The Indian victory was complete and bloody. The women were killed by driving their bodies into the ground with stakes. The men were scalped and their mouths filled with dirt—a symbol of the American greed for land. One survivor described the sight of scalped bodies strewn over the ground as resembling pumpkins scattered about a cornfield. A woman, in her haste to escape the Shawnee, threw her baby into a snow bank. In a paradoxical act of mercy, the Indians took the infant back to camp and raised it as their own.

Clearly, Washington needed a new general. To his disappointment, the best man available was Anthony Wayne, a former Revolutionary War commander. Washington described him as "a brave general and nothing else." Wayne was given a decimated fighting force, deathly scared of any Indian. At the same time, 22-year-old William Clark was promoted to lieutenant.

Meanwhile, the government pursued negotiations. Without delay, the Indians unceremoniously executed two U.S. peace commissioners. Undeterred, Washington invited a delegation of chiefs to the capital. John Bakeless, in his book, *Lewis and Clark: Partners in Discovery*, describes the conference this way: "(The chiefs) were received with the diplomatic protocol due ambassadors and dined with Washington. But as they promptly got drunk and persistently and joyfully stayed so, the cause of peace was not much advanced. Another peace conference at the mouth of the Detroit River lead to no better result, except that the diplomats managed to stay sober."

Wayne soon understood that negotiations would not solve the Indian problem. But instead of launching a quick retaliatory strike, he spent months drilling, disciplining, and organizing his troops. He established secure supply lines. He found reliable Indian scouts. In short, he did all the obvious things that his predecessors had failed to do. By the summer of 1794, Wayne was ready to attack.

During Wayne's preparations, Clark learned many skills that would become useful to him during the expedition. General Wayne sent Clark down the Ohio to spy on the Spanish. The Spanish were legitimately concerned about U.S. intentions on the frontier. They already knew that the French ambassador had asked George Rogers Clark to raise an army to attack the lower Mississippi. Now, here was his younger brother, traveling up and down the river, ostensibly on army business, but also making careful observations about Spanish troops and positions. The Spanish tried and failed to break into Clark's boat to learn his true purposes. This was fortunate. If they had succeeded, they might have found plans for all the Spanish river galleys and their armaments hidden inside. Clark spent the winter of 1793 much as he would spend the winters of 1804, 1805, and 1806: building a log fort and drilling the men inside.

The decisive battle with the Indians came in August of 1794. General Wayne tried to hide his true intentions by spreading rumors that he would move northwest against the Indian villages. Then, he spread a rumor that he would move northeast, towards the British Fort Miamis. Wayne marched toward the British and built his own fort nearby. His deceptions had fooled neither the Indians nor the British. The British were safely holed up in Fort Miamis. The Indians were fasting in preparation for battle. The forces finally met on August 20th. A small lead party of Kentuckians ran into the Indians, and immediately retreated into the main body. Briefly, confusion reigned. Then, the months of drilling paid off as Wayne's forces--including Clark--charged the Indians and sent them running to Fort Miamis for protection. Perhaps fearing U.S. reprisals, the British locked the gates and refused to admit even one Indian. The Indians never forgot this betrayal.

This left the British and Americans in an awkward situation. The Americans did not really want to attack a British fort. The British were more than a little chagrined to explain why there was a British fort in U.S. territory. Both sides postured and threatened and, in the end, walked away. Without any allies, the Indians decided to make peace with the U.S.

Lieutenant William Clark had served bravely, if perhaps a little too seriously to suit his comrades. One of the company clerks serving with Clark jokingly labeled their company's official records, *Company Book of Lt. Clark's & Wayne's Wars.*

After the victory over the Indians, General Wayne had Clark resume his spying on the Spanish. It was at this time that he refined his skills as a waterman and a mapmaker. Like many frontier settlers, Clark suffered intermittently from malaria. This sickness, along with his brother's financial problems, prompted him to resign from the army and return to Clarksville.

One day, a few years later, while Clark was in Virginia, he came upon two young girls who were struggling with their horse. It was too large for either of them to manage. He lead the horse on foot a short distance, then escorted the girls home. The girls were cousins: Julia (Judy) Hancock and Harriet Kennerly. There is a river in Montana named for Miss Hancock, who was later to become Mrs. Clark. After Julia's death, Clark would marry the other young rider, Harriet.

Chapter 12

From Clarksville to St. Louis

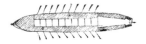

". . . one of the Shawnees a respectable looking Indian offered me three beverskins for my dog with which he appeared much pleased, the dog was of the Newfoundland breed one that I prised much for his docility and qualifications generally for my journey and of course there was no bargain . . ."

--Meriwether Lewis, November 16th, 1803, on an offer to sell his dog, "Seaman

The re-union of Lewis and Clark must have been a joyful affair. From their correspondence, it is clear that both men were thrilled to be the ones chosen to explore the continent, and they were thrilled to be doing it together. That night they had dinner with the man who might have preceded them, had he chose—George Rogers Clark. Years earlier, he had declined Jefferson's invitation to cross the continent. None of the men wrote about the meeting but we can surely guess what they discussed. What would the rivers be like? How

69

many men should they take? What skills would the men need to have? Would the Indians be friendly? When should they fight? When should they retreat?

They stayed almost two weeks in Clarksville making plans and selecting volunteers. Word had spread about the expedition, and men lined up to be included. They were looking for "some good hunters, stout, healthy, unmarried men, accustomed to the woods, and capable of bearing bodily fatigue in a pretty considerable degree." Lewis had brought John Colter and George Shannon along with him for Clark's approval. Clark had picked seven men for Lewis to approve. One of these was Charles Floyd. His father had served with George Rogers Clark during the Revolutionary War. Floyd and Nathaniel Pryor were made sergeants. The 12-man force that Congress had approved was quickly surpassed.

Clark also brought along a slave named York. York was Clark's manservant just as York's father had been a manservant for Clark's father. They were about the same age. York was young, strong, and healthy, an excellent addition to the party.

With the new members of the expedition, they headed down the Ohio to Fort Massac. Lewis expected to meet eight more volunteers here. They hadn't arrived. Rather than hold up the larger party, he hired a local frontiersman to locate the men and bring them to winter quarters near St. Louis. The man's name was George Drouillard, and he turned out to be one of the most valuable members of the party. His mother was Shawnee. His father was French-Canadian. This background made him an ideal interpreter. Drouillard also knew how to communicate with Indian sign language--a priceless skill as the expedition encountered tribes no U.S. citizen had ever met. Lewis hired him for $25 per month. In addition, he was an excellent hunter and comfortable with Indians. He quickly became Lewis' first choice for essential or difficult assignments.

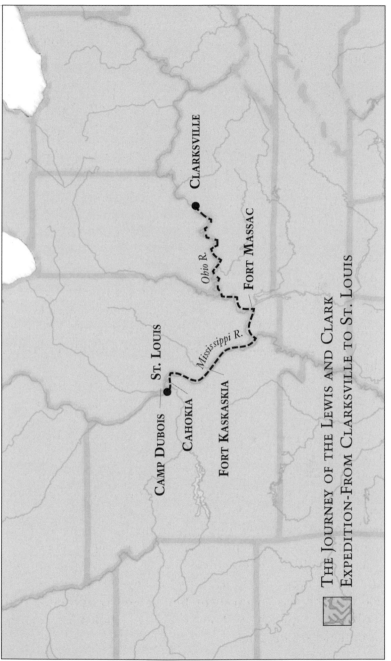

THE JOURNEY OF THE LEWIS AND CLARK
EXPEDITION-FROM CLARKSVILLE TO ST. LOUIS

From Ft. Massac it was only a two-day journey to the junction of the Mississippi and Ohio. They stopped at the mouth of the Ohio to practice celestial navigation. Lewis taught Clark the skills he had just recently learned in Philadelphia. Using an octant or a sextant to determine the angle of the sun, he could then determine latitude from a chart. Longitude was more difficult. Lewis' timepieces were not accurate enough to allow

Lewis respected Drouillard immensely but he never learned how to spell his name. In the journals, Lewis usually calls him "Drewyer." Sacajawea's husband Toussaint Charbonneau didn't fare well either. He is at different times referred to as, "Sharbono," "Charbono," "Chaubonie," or "Chabonah." Even Captain Clark was unable to escape 19th-Century spelling conventions unscathed. In the journal of his own sergeant, Patrick Gass, he is consistently called, "Captain Clarke."

such calculations so he did the next best thing. He noted the movement of the moon in relation to the stars. His journal is full of these measurements. When he returned, others would be able to use his measurements to determine exact longitude.

While Lewis and Clark were busy studying the stars and charting their exact location, the men were busy locating a place to buy whisky. Despite orders forbidding it, several men visited a trading post and got drunk. This was neither the first nor last incident of this type. It took a unique sort of man to qualify for the Corps of Discovery, as the members of the expedition came to be known. Youth, strength, and bravery were a given. They also had to be resourceful and independent enough to take care of themselves in the woods. They had to be a bit of a free spirit to be willing to leave all civilization behind and venture into the unknown wilderness. These traits didn't necessarily lend themselves to fitting into a cohesive military unit. The men would clearly need some severe discipline before they were ready to face the challenges of the west. Clark, in particular, was excellent at building such a united force. He would have made an excellent professor of organizational behavior, had such courses existed. Clark was able to strike the delicate balance between too much and too little discipline. He knew when to give the men an extra ration of whisky and when to inflict one hundred lashes. He knew when the men needed a break and when they needed a celebration. To peek ahead just a little, this group that could not even follow an order to stay sober, would later cheerfully follow the captains up a river which they believed, to a man, to be the wrong course.

The expedition started up the Mississippi on November 20th. Until this day, they had had the current of the Ohio pushing them along. From now until they reached the continental divide, the rivers would be fighting them every step of the way. Forcing a keelboat up the Mississippi and Missouri would be exhausting work. It is no coincidence that at this point, Lewis and Clark decided to double the size of the party.

It took four days to cover the first 48 miles to Cape Girardeau. Here they stopped to meet with the founder of the village, Louis Lorimier. When Lewis called, Lorimier was at a horse race. Lewis followed him there and was unimpressed with the spectacle. "The seane reminded me very much of their small raises in Kentucky among the uncivilized backwoodsmen, nor did the subsequent disorder which took place in consequences of the decision of the judges of the rase at all lessen the resembleance." He further described the participants as "men of desperate fortunes, but little to loose either character or property."

Lewis had a much higher opinion of Lorimier and his half-Shawnee daughter, whom he called "the most descent looking feemale I have seen since I left Louisville." Lorimier was a French-Canadian who had fought with the Indians against the colonies during the Revolution. He had even helped the Shawnees capture Daniel Boone. When George

Rogers Clark came through, he burned one of Lorimier's trading posts to the ground. Lorimier lost over $20,000 worth of merchandise. So ended his career as a merchant, but Lorimier did not hold grudges. That night, he welcomed Lewis to a festive dinner at his home.

This was an incredible loss for that time. Congress' initial appropriation for the entire Lewis and Clark expedition was only $2,500.

A few days later the expedition reached Fort Kaskaskia. They recruited more men, including two who would serve as sergeants, Patrick Gass and John Ordway. Gass was an excellent recruit for the picky captains. Although he was short—only 5' 7"— he was sturdily built. Gass was about the same age as Clark. Like Clark, he came from Indian country. When his father was drafted to protect the settlers, Patrick served in his place. He saw little fighting but learned valuable scouting skills. After his military service, he became a carpenter's apprentice, and worked on the house of James Buchanan, Sr, whose son became President of the United States. Lewis required skilled workmen, including carpenters. Within a few weeks they would need to build a fort somewhere near St. Louis.

Gass' commanding officer, Captain Russell Bissell, at Kaskaskia was none too pleased to be losing two of his best men. He flatly denied Gass permission to leave. Gass took a chance, going behind his commander's back, and arranged a private meeting with Lewis. It likely took little convincing to persuade Lewis of his value to the Corps of Discovery. Lewis met with Bissell and showed him his orders, signed by the President himself, allowing him to take any soldier he wanted anywhere he wanted. Nothing trumps a presidential order. Gass was allowed to go.

On December 4, Clark continued up the Mississippi with the men by boat while Lewis went ahead by horseback. By the 8th, he was in St. Louis and meeting with the Spanish governor, Colonel Carlos Dehault Delassus. The Spanish were not at all happy to see Captain Lewis. As far as Delassus was concerned, there was no advantage to his country in Lewis' foray up the Missouri. Already, American settlers were pouring into Spanish territory and undermining the territorial claims of Spain. Just as Jefferson had suggested to foreign

Colonel Carlos Dehault Delassus, Spanish Governor of Louisiana. Courtesy of the Missouri Historical Society.

75

diplomats in Washington, Lewis now told the governor that the mission was a purely scientific enterprise. He would map the country and bring back useful information to share with all countries. Delassus was not a fool. Lewis' half-truth was no more credible in St. Louis than when Jefferson told it in Washington. In a report to his superiors, Delassus noted that: "According to advices, I believe that his mission has no other object than to discover the Pacific Ocean, following the Missouri, and to make intelligent observations, because he has the reputation of being a very well educated man and of many talents."

Still, Louisiana would be American territory in a few weeks. There was little Delassus could do to stop Lewis, but he could slow him down. He denied permission for the expedition to proceed up the Missouri until the formal transfer of territory had taken place. This would have been the perfect opportunity for Lewis to set out on his adventure to the Southwest. Instead, fortunately for Jefferson, Lewis decided to camp for the winter near St. Louis. Perhaps the obvious antagonism of the Spanish governor made him re-evaluate his plan to explore in their holdings, or maybe he just realized that he had plenty do that winter in St. Louis. He still needed to recruit more soldiers. Lewis envisioned a party four times the size of the original 12-man force. There would be additional supplies to procure. The keelboat needed some modifications. This would also be his last chance to correspond with Jefferson before he passed outside the parameters of the U.S. postal service.

The Spanish also had time to plan. They had no intention of allowing Lewis and Clark to successfully complete their mission. They knew Lewis was lying about the purpose of his mission. Maybe he was laying the groundwork for a U.S. takeover of Texas and New Mexico. Maybe the U.S. would even invade Mexico. Clark's older brother had been ready to attempt that very thing just ten years before. Among the

Spanish authorities, Lewis was secretly referred to as "Captain Merry," and a plot to foil his mission was being planned. Nemesio Salcedo, Commandant-General of the Interior Provinces of New Spain wrote: "Nothing would be more useful than the apprehension of Merry, and even though I realize it is not an easy undertaking, chance might proportion things in such a way that it might be successful." The Spanish would enlist the help of the Comanches. With a little luck, they would catch the small party on their way up the Missouri.

Chapter 13

Frontier St. Louis

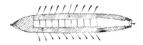

"For of all the rivers that were destiny to St. Louis, those that flowed from the wilderness counted most, the French had pioneered them, and the town polarized innumerable energies from the eastward in order to direct them west. Here was the headland from which the nation overlooked the West. The Ohio and the lower Mississippi were important, but the upper Mississippi meant more and the Missouri most of all. The Indians and trappers and voyageurs who brought a barbaric color to the cobbled streets were of the West, and an old and rich aristocracy, dating back long before Mr. Jefferson's Purchase, were borne on their shoulders."

--Bernard DeVoto, *Across the Wide Missouri*

It is worth pausing for a moment here to examine the city that Lewis and Clark saw in December of 1803, and where they spent nearly six months making their final preparations for the journey. Although the population was only a thousand people, St. Louis was the center of commerce for the western economy. It was the last opportunity to buy supplies for settlers and traders heading west, and it was the eastern trading post for Indians and trappers returning to sell furs. In many respects it was like a gold rush town. Instead of gold, the precious commodity was fur. Goods and services were exchanged based not on dollars or francs but beaver skins.

Jefferson had asked Lewis to gather as much statistical information as he could about St. Louis and the Missouri territory. He started his enquiries with the Spanish surveyor general, Antoine Soulard. Soulard had census data from 1800 that counted 10,000 inhabitants in Upper Louisiana, not including Indians, of course. Two-thirds were white, consisting mainly of French-Canadians, but also Spaniards and a few Americans. Most of the rest were black slaves. Both the white and slave populations were growing every day. St. Louis was becoming the western melting pot of the United States. Any number of languages might be heard on the streets including Indian dialects. One result of the melting pot was a large number half French-half Indian children, who became known as "Métis." Much like the royalty of Europe, leading French and Indian families would sometimes deliberately intermarry to strengthen ties between important financial partners. The Métis served a valuable role as translators of both language and culture. Lewis also recognized the value of the Métis. Three of his most skilled frontiersmen were George Drouillard, Pierre Cruzatte, and Francois Labiche—all of French and Indian ancestry.

Soon there would be even more languages spoken in St. Louis. On March 9, 1804, when Colonel Delassus and Captain Amos Stoddard put their signatures to the document that would officially transfer possession of Louisiana to the U.S., the floodgates of migration would open—and not just for Americans. Europeans would immigrate by the thousands to help fill up the land. Jefferson hoped that the trans-Mississippi west could be kept free as an Indian preserve, where they might learn to farm and become good Americans. Before Louisiana was even purchased, American settlers had rendered that plan unworkable.

Lewis made another valuable contact in St. Louis. His name was James Mackay. Mackay had traveled up the Missouri as far as the Platte River. His assistant had made it all the way to the Mandan Villages in present North Dakota. Based on these travels, Mackay had drawn a map of the Missouri River. Lewis was able to sit down with him and learn what he knew and what he had heard.

The merchants in St. Louis had to be thrilled to see Lewis. With his unexpectedly enlarged force, he had only a fraction of what he needed. He could hardly go back to Philadelphia for supplies. The merchants had a captive market and they knew it. Further, he had an unlimited line of credit signed by the President of the United States. In sales terms, he was a qualified prospect.

Two trading companies were vying for his business, one owned by Manuel Lisa, the other by Pierre and Auguste Chouteau. The Chouteaus were two of the earliest and richest residents of St. Louis. Unlike their unfortunate former competitor, Louis Lorimier, the Chouteaus had picked the winning side in the Revolutionary War. Rather than being burned out by George Rogers Clark, he made them his trading partners. For over twenty years, the Chouteaus enjoyed a trade monopoly. They were a frontier version of Wal-Mart, selling everything a farmer or trapper might need--food, guns, hardware, clothing, and more—without a competitor in sight. They also bought furs, which were then re-sold at a handsome profit on the east coast and Europe.

In 1798, Manuel Lisa arrived in St. Louis, and provided the Chouteaus with an adversary worthy of their talents. He once wrote, "I go a great distance while some are considering whether they will start today or tomorrow." Lisa had the advantage of being a Spanish citizen and, thus, was

Manuel Lisa. Courtesy of the Missouri Historical Society.

able to procure land grants based on the fiction that he was going to become a farmer. He lost no time setting up his own trading business, but he had one major obstacle to overcome. The Spanish government had already awarded the Chouteaus the exclusive license to trade with the Osage Indians. Lisa argued fervently and articulately that the Indian trade should be open to all comers, a position he no doubt believed passionately right up until the day in 1802 when he finagled a way to win the exclusive Osage trade rights for himself.

Lewis and Clark provided an immediate, temporary stimulus to the St. Louis economy. But there was hope of much more among the merchants. If the expedition returned—with an accurate map and knowledge of the new territory—Lisa and the Chouteaus would be ready to expand the fur trade and make themselves even richer.

Chapter 14

Waiting at Camp Wood

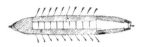

*"(Private John) S(hields). opposeds order & has threttened
(Sergeant John)Od (Ordways')—Life, wishes to return."*

--William Clark, undated, winter 1804

When the Spanish refused Lewis permission to continue
up the Missouri, he decided to build a winter camp near St.
Louis. A friendly fur trader named Nicholas Jarrot offered
the party his property near the mouth of the Wood River, on
the U.S. side of the Mississippi. Clark continued with the
men upriver to the campsite and started building their winter
quarters directly across from the Missouri. Lewis stayed in St.
Louis to buy supplies and gather information.

Drouillard arrived a few days behind Clark with the eight
Tennessee recruits. As at Fort Massac, Lewis was
unimpressed with the quality of the volunteers. He sent them
on to Clark, where only four of the men made the final cut.

Clark had a few important tasks to complete. He built a

This map, taken from a Samuel Lewis sketch based on William Clark's original drawings, shows the location of St. Louis and Wood River. The expedition built their camp at the mouth of the Wood River, directly across from the confluence of the Mississippi and Missouri Rivers. Courtesy of the Library of Congress, Geography and Map Division.

fort. He also made some clever renovations to the keelboat. Lockers were added along the sides of the boat for storage. The lockers protected vital supplies but they could also be raised as shields during a skirmish. With the lids down, men could walk along the sides of the boat as they poled upriver. Clark also added benches for oarsmen and center poles for additional sails. Rumors about the hostility of the Teton Sioux spurred Clark to fortify the boat even further. He mounted a cannon on a swivel that allowed it to be fired in any direction. In a close battle, one shot could kill or wound a dozen Indians or more. This was a weapon sure to impress any tribe. As if that were not enough, he mounted two large shotguns, called "blunderbusses," on the ship's stern. Clark effectively transformed a cargo vessel into a battleship.

By presenting such an obvious show of force, the captains ran the risk of being perceived as conquerors rather than explorers and mapmakers. After some discussion they probably realized that the Indians would be no more gullible than the Europeans. No intelligent observer was going to believe the expedition was a purely scientific venture. They were the new possessors of the land. The Indians were their subjects. Why not try to impress them at the outset with an awesome show of American power and technology? Lewis and Clark decided to meet the Indians in full military dress, present their men in drill formations, and shoot off a few rounds with the mysterious air gun. Would the Indians be impressed by their new "Great Father"? Would they dare to fight the Corps of Discovery and take their enormous armament? Time would tell. Meanwhile, the men were fighting among themselves.

Clark tried to keep the soldiers busy at Camp Wood. They drilled every day. They had target practice. But once the huts were built and the keelboat was finished, there was little real work to do. While Lewis, and occasionally Clark, were off in St. Louis hobnobbing at balls and picnics with the glitterati (such as they were in a frontier town), the men were bored stiff. Their only diversion was alcohol, which the commanding officers tried unsuccessfully to control. In reality, Lewis and Clark had done an excellent job of picking soldiers. The problem was that the best candidates were young men who longed for adventure, not men who were content to spend months performing military drills in a tiny fort. The men of the Corps of Discovery acted exactly as should have been expected. They started complaining, drinking, fighting, wandering off, and becoming insubordinate. Clark, being a skilled commander, was able to maintain order but Sergeant Ordway was not as fortunate.

When Lewis returned to camp, Ordway made a disturbing report. Reubin Field and John Shields disobeyed a direct order to assume guard duty, flatly refusing to take commands from anyone but the captains. John Colter, John Boley, Peter Weiser, and John Robinson at least had the sense not to flaunt their disobedience. They told Ordway they were going hunting, then found a whisky seller and got drunk. Given Lewis' temper, he must have been furious. His mood is readily apparent in the tone of a detachment order he had read to all the men on March 3rd.

"The commanding officer feels himself mortifyed and disappointed at the disorderly conduct of Reubin Fields . . . nor is he less surprised at the want of discretion in those who urged his opposition to the faithfull discharge of his duty, particularly Shields . . ."

Lewis goes on to explain what should have been obvious to the men upon a "moments reflection"—that he and Clark could not possibly remain continuously at camp so that the men would obey orders. Lewis confined the quartet of drunk "hunters" to quarters for ten days.

The detachment order didn't work. A month later Shields disobeyed Ordway's orders again and, this time, threatened to kill him. About the same time, Colter became angry about an order and loaded his gun, intending to shoot Ordway. Shields and Colter were tried for mutiny on March 29th. Both men asked forgiveness and were released with the promise to "doe better in the future." Colter even remained in Ordway's Third Squad. This seems an incredibly light sentence given their earlier insubordination. Perhaps Clark understood the men's frustration in having to wait for months to get underway. His patience was well rewarded, as Colter and Shields both distinguished themselves during the expedition. Meanwhile, Sergeant Ordway was probably looking forward to fighting some Indians so the men's anger and guns would be pointed in another direction.

Everyone in camp eagerly anticipated April 18th, the date they would finally get out of Camp Wood, push their boats across the Mississippi, and begin their voyage up the Missouri—the river that had been staring them in the face since December. A few days before the 18th, Lewis delivered the bad news. He needed more time to prepare. There were still supplies he required. He also had to make arrangements for an Osage chief to visit Jefferson with Pierre Chouteau. The men would have to wait another month. Surely, there was a collective groan from the men as the news was announced.

Lewis went on a tremendous buying spree--shirts, flour, corn, salt, pork, soap—well over $1,000 in a week. He had the foresight to buy mosquito netting, and the wisdom to buy whisky (120 gallons). Whisky would be popular with the Indians and, of course, the men. If used sparingly, there would be enough alcohol to last until the men were too far up the river to desert.

Despite all the money Lewis had pumped into the St. Louis economy, Manuel Lisa was unhappy with his share, which was substantial. Lisa threatened to complain to the American Governor in New Orleans that Lewis had treated him unfairly. Lewis was incensed. On May 6, he wrote a letter to Clark.

"Damn Manuel, And triply Damn Mr. B (Lisa's partner, Francis Benoit). They give me more vexation and trouble than their lives are worth. I have dealt very plainly with these gentlemen, in short I have come to an open rupture with them; I think them both great scoundrels.

These gentlemen (gentlemen is crossed out), these puppies, are not unacquainted with my opinions. . . . strange indeed, that men to appearance in their senses, will manifest such strong symptoms of insanity as to be whetting knives to cut their own throats."

That was not the worst of the news. The Secretary of War had sent a letter to Lewis confirming Clark's commission. Lewis had promised Clark a co-command and the rank of captain equal to his own. Secretary Dearborn tersely noted that, "The peculiar situation, circumstances, and orginisation of the Corps of Engineers is such as would render the appointment of Mr. Clark a Captain in that Corps improper." Lewis was horrified. His honor was on the line, something he did not take lightly. There was not time to appeal to the President for a remedy, so he did the only honorable thing he could. He kept Clark's rank a secret. For the entire journey, only Clark and Lewis knew that Clark was a lieutenant while Captain Lewis was his superior officer. Clark agreed to the pretense.

This moment gives us considerable insight into the personality and friendship of Lewis and Clark. Lewis seems not the least bit interested in exploiting the situation to his advantage. Clark was clearly committed to the venture. Lewis could have broken the bad news, apologized for forces beyond his control, and assumed command. Clark would have acquiesced. The credit and glory would have belonged to Lewis alone. There is no indication that he pondered this for even a moment. He wanted a shared command. Theirs was truly a remarkable friendship. How rare that two such capable and ambitious men could so willingly agree to share the responsibilities and rewards of such a prestigious undertaking. Neither man suffered from the petty jealousies that would certainly have occurred in lesser men. Clark's response is also instructive. He knew that in point of fact Lewis was his commanding officer and could assume command at any time or overrule any decision Clark might make along the way. Clark was in what most military men would consider an emasculated position. Yet he went ahead anyway. He trusted Lewis to treat him as an equal regardless of the blunders of some paper-pushers in Washington. His trust in Lewis was absolute and unwavering, and his trust was not misplaced. Throughout the journey, Lewis never tried to assert authority over Clark in any way. In fact, there is no record of the captains even having a serious disagreement. The issue was never raised again until Lewis returned to St. Louis over two years later and immediately wrote the President a letter insisting that Clark be given credit and rewards equal to his own.

On May 14th, the long wait was finally over. The Corps of Discovery was ready to start up the Missouri. Sergeant Ordway could have been speaking for the whole group when he wrote excitedly to his parents: "We are to ascend the Missouri River with a boat as far as it is navigable and then go by land to the western ocean, if nothing prevents . . . We expect to be gone 18 months or two years. We are to Receive a great Reward for this expedition, when we Return. If we make Great Discoveries as we expect, the united States, has promised to make us Great Rewards more than we are promised."

Chapter 15

The Journals

"Lewis and Clark were the writingest explorers of their time. They wrote constantly and abundantly, afloat and ashore, legibly and illegibly, and always with an urgent sense of purpose."

--Donald Jackson

In 985 A.D., Bjarni Herjolfson was sailing from Iceland to Greenland. His ship was blown off course and he finally made landfall in modern Newfoundland. Herjolfson thus became the first European to set foot on the North American continent. Fifteen years later, Leif Ericsson followed his route and became the second. If either Ericsson or Herjolfson had had the foresight to keep a daily journal of their adventures, we might be celebrating Ericsson Day or Bjarni's Birthday instead of Columbus Day.

Fame doesn't always come to the most deserving. Sometimes it comes to the man with the best publicist. Lewis was not unaware of this truth. He instructed Clark and all three sergeants to keep a journal. He knew they would be making history, but making history is irrelevant if nobody reads about it. Looking back two centuries later, the single most enduring accomplishment of the Lewis and Clark expedition may well be the publication of the journals. Yes, they were the first Americans to explore the continent to the Pacific and they deserve recognition for that, but they were not indispensable. Even on their way home they came across dozens of traders and trappers headed the other direction, on their way to the beaver dams of the Missouri. In retrospect, Lewis and Clark were not leaders influencing settlers to come to the new lands; they were the very tip of a vast wave of American and European settlement that would eventually inundate the West. Right or wrong, America had a manifest destiny to populate the continent, and they would do it with or without Lewis and Clark. Lewis and Clark are special not because they opened the west. They are special because they wrote down their adventures. We know about their first encounters with the Sioux, the grizzly, and the Rocky Mountains. We have that rare opportunity to understand them as men, not just explorers or legends. Without the journals, "Lewis and Clark" might well be an answer to a trivia question.

For all their importance, there are many mysteries surrounding the journals. When were they written? We're not sure. From internal evidence and by comparison between the different authors, it appears that sometimes they were written during the evening after the day's adventures. Sometimes they were composed weeks or months later based on hastily written field notes. Given the large degree of agreement and similar language between the different journals, it seems apparent that the authors compared notes to keep their stories straight. The biggest mystery is why Lewis himself failed to keep a regular record. He was the expedition's best-educated and most descriptive writer. He was personally instructed by Jefferson to keep a journal. He issued the orders requiring the sergeants to maintain their own journals, yet there are longs gaps--almost a year in one case--where Lewis fails to write a single word. How could a man who had the initiative and energy to plan and execute an expedition across the continent fail to spend a few minutes each day to write about it? There are no good explanations. Stephen Ambrose speculates that Lewis may have been depressed. By Jefferson's admission, he was subject to "melancholy." But why would his depression allow him to fulfill all his other duties so admirably and affect only his writing? Clark notes that some of the journals were lost when a pirogue nearly overturned. Perhaps a year of Lewis' journals ended up floating down the Missouri. The least likely but most hopeful explanation is that the journals have been temporarily lost. One day, to the delight of historians, a lucky St. Louis housewife may find a few dusty volumes long hidden in her attic.

The journal authors were writing at the direction of Thomas Jefferson, and the President's interests were purely practical and scientific. Thus, the journal entries tend to be matter of fact about events that scream out for further commentary. Clark, in particular, rarely discusses his emotions or reflections about any aspect of the voyage. At one turning point in the expedition, Clark stood in one of the pirogues arguing with an Indian chief about the quantity of presents to be delivered. The chief's warriors refused to let the pirogue return to the keelboat. Clark insisted. Lewis loaded and aimed the cannon. Dozens of Indians strung their bows and pointed them at Clark. At a moment when most men would be shaking with fear, Clark merely wrote, "I felt myself warm & spoke in verry positive terms."

Lewis also understated emotions, almost to the point of hilarity. The men, at first, were fascinated by the Indians' tales of large bears. After the first few encounters with grizzlies, which resulted in the men hiding in trees and jumping into rivers to save their lives, Lewis subtly remarks that, "I find that the curiossity of our party is pretty well satisfyed with rispect to this anamal."

Simply based on the journals, we know maddeningly little about the character and personality of Lewis and Clark. We know even less, barely anything at all in most instances, about the other men and woman who comprised the Corps of Discovery. As a hunter and interpreter, George Drouillard was perhaps as vital to the success of the expedition as Lewis and Clark. After Clark, he was Lewis' most trusted advisor and lieutenant, yet we have no idea why Lewis relied on him. Was he brave? Was he wise? The journals don't equip us to make those types of judgments. York must have been thrilled to be treated as "big medicine" by the Indians instead of as a slave by the whites, but Clark never bothers to provide any details of York's service or thoughts, so we can never know his perspective. Indeed, Lewis and Clark rarely bother to discuss the attitudes of any of the party, other than to say they were in low or high spirits.

The one notable exception is Sacajawea's husband, Toussaint Charbonneau. Lewis described him as a "man of no peculiar merit." After he caused the boating accident in which some of the journals were lost, Lewis called him "perhaps the most timid waterman in the world." No other member of the party received as much attention—positive or negative—as their French interpreter.

One final comment is necessary on Clark's technical deficiencies as a writer. Lewis and Clark scholar Robert Betts dryly observes that Clark "was not only the master misspeller of them all, but also displayed dazzling virtuosity in his approach to punctuation, capitalization, and simple sentence structure." He was not even consistent in his mistakes. He spelled "Sioux" 27 different ways, including my personal favorite, "Cocoux." Clark capitalizes words, at any point in a sentence, in a totally random manner. Professor Donald Jackson tried to work out some pattern to his capitalization but he ultimately "retired in confusion." In Clark's defense, we should remember that some of the best educated Americans of the time—even Jefferson--commonly made spelling errors. At the turn of the 19th Century, spelling was just in the process of being standardized by men like Noah Webster.

There is a temptation, in light of all of the blatant spelling and grammatical errors, to assume that Lewis and Clark were not smart men. Nothing could be further from the truth. In some respects they were not well educated but their native intelligence is beyond dispute. Lewis' scientific observations are insightful. Clark's accomplishments as a geographer are extraordinary. The very fact that the expedition succeeded proves they were men of great resourcefulness. Foolish men did not last long in the wilderness. In his introduction to the journals, Bernard DeVoto writes: "Both were men of great intelligence, of distinguished intelligence. The entire previous history of North American exploration contains no one who could be considered their intellectual equal."

Chapter 16

Up the Missouri

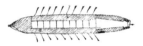

"The best authenticated accounts informed us, that we were to pass through a country possessed by numerous, powerful, and warlike nations of savages, of gigantic stature, fierce, treacherous and cruel; and particularly hostile to white men."

--Sergeant Patrick Gass, May 14, 1804

On May 14, 1804, at 4:00 PM, in the midst of "hard showers of rain," the Corps of Discovery finally left Camp Wood. A few citizens turned out to watch them depart, and the crew fired the keelboat cannon in celebration. Twenty-two privates, three sergeants, and the captains manned the keelboat. They were accompanied by two pirogues. One was manned by Corporal Richard Warfington and six soldiers; the other by eight French voyagers. The captains planned to take these two smaller boats as far as the Mandan Villages. The crews of the pirogues would then return to St. Louis with the keelboat.

95

The keelboat and pirogues were filled with every item that Lewis and Clark thought useful. They took carpenter, blacksmithing, and medical tools, scientific instruments, twenty barrels of flour, seven barrels of salt, fifty kegs of pork, and fifty bushels of meal. There were 21 bales of trade goods for the Indians, each carefully sorted and organized to be used at the proper time. The boats were loaded nearly to capacity, yet Clark ominously noted that the supplies were "not as much as I think ness (esary)."

Once the expedition started up the Missouri, they would be in territory familiar to only a tiny group of white men. After the Mandan Villages they would be in completely unknown country. There would be no opportunity to buy more supplies or ask for additional instructions. Lewis and Clark would be like Columbus, sailing across undiscovered, mysterious, and perilous waters.

Only one member of the crew was missing—Captain Lewis. He had final arrangements to make with Pierre Chouteau who was taking a group of Osage chiefs back to Washington D.C. to visit President Jefferson. That was his official explanation. He was also saying good-bye to his many friends and admirers in St. Louis, almost exclusively female. After some difficult duty attending various balls and picnics, Lewis eventually joined Clark by horseback, about fifteen miles upriver, in St. Charles.

Lewis was not the only one craving a last opportunity to mingle with women. In St. Charles, the town hosted a ball for the men. Clark declined to attend but noted nonchalantly, that "Seven Ladies visit me to day." Sergeant Ordway sensed trouble. In a detachment order signed by Clark, but written by Ordway, the men are warned to "have a true respect for their own Dignity and not make it necessary for him (Capt. Clark) to leave St. Charles—for a more retired Situation—" As usual, Ordway was right. Private John Collins acted in an "unbecoming manner at the ball." The journals say no more

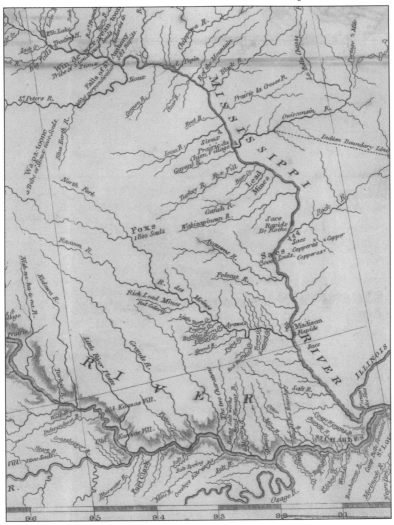

William Clark map of the first leg of the journey from St. Louis. Courtesy of the Library of Congress, Geography and Map Division.

than that but if Collins' past--and future--are any guide, his behavior probably included heavy drinking followed by arguing and fighting. Back at camp, he made a bad situation worse by disparaging the captain's orders and disappearing for the night along with two other men, William Warner and Hugh Hall.

The next day, Ordway presided over a court-martial for the three men. Warner and Hall plead guilty to being absent without leave and were sentenced to 25 lashes, with a recommendation of mercy based on past good behavior. Collins plead guilty to being AWOL but not guilty to being disorderly at the ball and disrespectful to orders at camp. He was found guilty on all three counts. Clark suspended the sentence on Warner and Hall but allowed Collins to receive fifty lashes on his bare back. This type of corporal punishment was common in the army at that time. Collins would be sore but still able to row the keelboat. The other men would see the consequences of undisciplined behavior and, hopefully, be deterred. The sentence was carried out at sunset using either switches or the ramrods from the men's guns, not the heavy leather whips used by the British navy and some slave owners. That type of lashing might have been fatal.

On Sunday, several of the men celebrated mass at the local Catholic Church. The following afternoon, May 21, they departed St. Charles. Two days later, Captain Lewis very nearly fell to his death. Clark was with the boat. Lewis was walking alone alongside the river, searching for new plants and animals. This became a common pattern throughout the journey. Lewis was on a bluff, about 300 feet above the river. Somehow he lost his footing and started plummeting toward the river. After falling down the slope about twenty feet, he was able to stop himself by digging into the precipice with his knife. A less modest man might have embellished the story and bragged about his resourcefulness and bravery. These were the types of stories that made mountain men like Jim Bridger, Jedediah Smith, and John Colter (a member of the Corps of Discovery) into legends. That wasn't Lewis' style. He was a reserved Southern gentleman. The incident is not even recorded in his journal. Clark gives it only two succinct lines.

The same day, the expedition passed Boone's settlement, where Daniel Boone lived in a 4-story Georgian mansion. In 1804, he would have been almost seventy years old. Private Joseph Whitehouse wrote that Boone had "discover'd Kentucky" and was "residing at this place, with a number of his family and friends." Boone had led the settlement of Kentucky twenty years earlier, but had left when it became "too crowded" for his taste. Now he lived even further west, at the extreme edge of American settlement. Boone would have had a wealth of knowledge about the river, local Indians, and game. But if Lewis and Clark had the chance to discuss these issues with the famous explorer, it didn't make it into the journals. As Lewis' near-death experience on the riverbank merited only a couple lines, perhaps Daniel Boone

If the Lewis and Clark expedition had occurred thirty years earlier, Daniel Boone would have been the logical leader. He helped find and build the trails that led west to Kentucky. Later, he became one of the first settlers, founding Boonesborough, Kentucky. The Shawnees joined with the British during the Revolutionary War to expel the new white settlers. Boone's daughter was kidnapped during the fighting, but he was able to track the Shawnee warriors. During a surprise attack he rescued her and two other young girls. When Kentucky was made a state, Boone was unable to prove a clear title to the lands he had settled, and lost them all. He decided to relocate in Missouri, where Lewis and Clark passed him in 1804. After the Louisiana Purchase, Boone's farm became American territory instead of Spanish. Creditors from Kentucky took the occasion to sue Boone for old debts and, once again, he lost all of his land. He stayed in St. Charles where he died in 1820 at the age of 85.

warranted none at all.

The expedition reached the last white settlement, La Charette, on May 25th. Here they met a French trader named Regis Loisel. Lewis already knew of Loisel from acquaintances in St. Louis. He and his partner, Pierre Antoine Tabeau, had been trying to set up a fur trading business that would compete with the British companies from Canada. They had just built a fort in Sioux country, near present Pierre, South Dakota. The Sioux were closely aligned with the British and wanted little to do with French or American traders, but at least they still had their scalps. That could almost be interpreted as a sign of goodwill among the Teton Sioux. Loisel was friendly with Lewis and Clark, and the captains were able to gather some useful information. However, Loisel's information came at a price. He also asked questions and tried to learn what he could about the mission of the Corps of Discovery. A few days later he would be in St. Louis, and later, New Orleans, exciting already nervous Spanish authorities about American intentions to claim land on the Pacific. Loisel lobbied for a position as a Spanish Indian agent but his warnings about American territorial aspirations had much larger repercussions. Soon, officials in Madrid would learn of the Lewis and Clark expedition and Spanish forces would be on their way to stop them.

Forcing their way up the Missouri, the men of the Corps of Discovery had much smaller concerns than geo-political restructuring. Each day brought new challenges. On June 4th, the mast of the keelboat caught on an overhanging tree and snapped. The expedition was forced to stop and construct a replacement. Once they were underway, they had a near disaster. The stern of the keelboat caught on a snag. The current of the river swung the ship around, presenting an unavoidable target for the gigantic logs—some as large as four feet in diameter—floating down the river. According to Clark, "This was a disagreeable and Dangerous Situation, particularly as immense large trees were Drifting down and we lay immediately in their Course." The men acted without hesitation. They grabbed ropes and swam ashore. Quickly, and with great exertion, they swung the keelboat out of danger. Obstacles large and small persisted. Clark's slave, York, nearly lost an eye when a fellow voyager threw sand at him. On June 23rd, the wind was so great that the party was forced to remain camped on an island the entire day. The weather nearly destroyed the boats again on July 14th. The expedition had gone about a mile in hard rain and moderate wind when the sky suddenly blackened. The keelboat was trapped between the tip of a sandy island and a dangerous shoreline, lined with snags. A furious wind came up. Again, the men tried to secure the boat with ropes to keep it from being "thrown up on the Sand Island, and dashed to pieces." Waves began washing over the side of the boat, and would likely have filled the hull and sunk the boat had it not been for one of Clark's modifications. The lockers he had built along the sides of the boats helped deflect some of the water. For forty minutes the men battled the storm. Then the storm disappeared, and within "1 minit the river was as Smooth as glass."

The Corps of Discovery was the first scientific expedition to ascend the Missouri, but there were a few trappers and traders who had preceded them. They had already passed Loisel on the river, and Lewis had visited with James Mackay in St. Louis. Now they were meeting small parties that were on their way back to St. Louis to sell their goods. Two trappers had gone up the Kansas River and had a successful season, only to lose all of their beaver pelts to a prairie fire. Another group had been as far as Sioux country. They had been out for nearly a year. All of their supplies and powder were exhausted but their canoe was loaded with $900 worth of furs. According to Stephen Ambrose, in *Undaunted Courage*, this was "about as profitable a venture as any young ambitious entrepreneur could find, other than a gold or silver claim." He also notes that the $900 would be multiplied by a factor of ten when the furs were re-sold in New York, and again multiplied by ten when they were sold in China. Before gold was discovered in California and South Dakota, beaver was the commodity that fueled dreams of quick riches in the West.

The expedition met another party on June 12th, headed by Pierre Dorion. Dorion worked as an interpreter at Loisel's trading post among the Sioux. He must also have done some trading himself as he had one boat loaded with furs and another with supplies. Twenty years earlier, Dorion had married a Sioux woman and made his permanent home among them. Naturally, he was fluent in Sioux, as well as French and English. The captains stayed up late that night swapping stories. As with so many other players in the Lewis and Clark saga, Dorion knew George Rogers Clark. They had corresponded back in 1780. Even here, at the extreme edge of the explored portion of the North American continent, William Clark was still in the shadow of his famous older brother. Clark seems unaffected by fraternal jealousy but he must have longed for the day when he would return to the states as a heroic explorer and finally be viewed as his brother's equal. Eventually the captains persuaded Dorion to join them, at least as far as the villages of the Yankton Sioux, where he was known and respected. They also entertained hopes that Dorion could persuade a delegation of Sioux chiefs to visit President Jefferson.

From the end of June through the beginning of August, the Corps of Discovery faced its most difficult disciplinary challenges. Lewis and Clark had tried to be lenient with the men while they were in settled territory but now military order was a necessity. Every man had to rely absolutely on the dependability of his fellow soldiers, whether it was watching for Indians at night or watching for snags and drifting logs

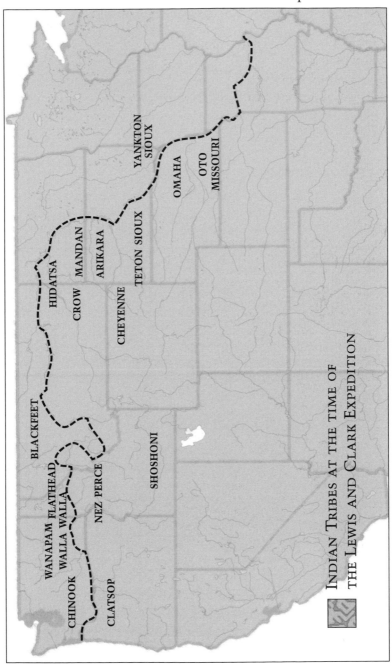

INDIAN TRIBES AT THE TIME OF
THE LEWIS AND CLARK EXPEDITION

during the day. A mistake in judgment could be fatal.

The first mistake came on June 29th. Private John Collins was on guard duty. To this point, Collins was the only man who had been lashed for any offense, and as such he should have known better. While everyone was asleep during Collins' nighttime guard duty, he broke into the whisky supply and got drunk. Hugh Hall found him first. Instead of reporting Collins, Hall helped himself to the whisky as well. This was a particularly foolish offense by both men. Of course, a drunken sentry is of little use. Indians might have easily raided the camp while Collins was incapacitated. Collins and Hall had also committed a serious offense against their fellow soldiers. There was a limited supply of whisky. Every man received a small share at dinner. Every man also knew that the whisky would run out sometime in the next few months. Each ounce that Collins and Hall drank that night was a portion that they stole from men on whom they depended for their very lives and by whom they would be judged the next day at court-martial. Collins plead not guilty but was convicted anyway. He had no effective defense to present. Hall, perhaps hoping for mercy, plead guilty. The court gave Collins one hundred lashes and Hall fifty. Lewis and Clark did not serve on the court-martial. They didn't need to. Clark noted insightfully that the men were "always found verry ready to punish Such Crimes." That was the last time anyone tried stealing whisky.

Two weeks later the captains convened another court-martial. This time a guilty verdict could mean death. Private Alexander Hamilton Willard was charged with "Lying down and Sleeping on his post whilst a Sentinal, on the night of the 11th." Sergeant Ordway, who often seemed to be in the middle of these disciplinary problems, had discovered Willard and turned him in. At the court-martial, Willard admitted that he had lain down but denied that he was asleep. No doubt, the captains were not overly concerned with such minor distinctions. Willard had committed this offense at an unfortunate time. Just two nights before, the men had seen a fire on the opposite shore while they were camped. When they went to investigate, the fire mysteriously went out. This appeared to be a sure sign of Indians. The men sprang into action, preparing for a Sioux war party. The cannon was fired as a warning to the Sioux and to alert all of the men. Nothing happened. The next morning the mysterious fire was found to be a small group of the Corps of Discovery. They had not heard the search party because of the wind. Still, the men knew that hostile Indians were out there and that their only protection might be Private Willard, who might be fast asleep. After deliberation, Lewis and Clark decided to let Willard live. They ordered him to receive a hundred lashes, spread out over four nights. Once again, the men received the message. There were no more reports of sleeping sentries.

The third and most serious offense occurred in the first part of August. Moses Reed told the captains he had left a knife at a previous campsite. He was allowed to return and retrieve it. When he failed to come back after three days, the captains concluded that he had deserted. This was one offense that absolutely could not be tolerated. They were headed into Sioux territory. They would need every gun available. The captains decided to send another message. They gave Drouillard orders to find Reed and bring him back—"dead or alive." He was also to find one of the French voyagers, appropriately named "La Liberte," whom they also feared had deserted. Drouillard left immediately with three men. He was the party's most skilled hunter. Now he would be tracking quarry of a much different nature.

The Corps of Discovery celebrated the 4th of July, 1804, by firing the cannon and naming a nearby stream, "Independence Creek." Even though the day consisted mainly of another typical struggle against the Missouri, Clark broke from his usual, matter-of-fact writing style and waxed poetic about the beauty of the land he was seeing for the first time. The country described would be near the present town of Doniphan, Kansas, about fifty miles north of Kansas City.

"The Plains of this countrey are covered with a Leek Green Grass, well calculated for the sweetest and most nourishing hay –interspersed with Cops (copses) of trees, Spreding ther lofty branchs over Pools Springs or Brooks of fine water. Groops of Shrubs covered with the most delicious froot is to be seen in every direction, and nature appears to have exerted herself to butify the Senery by the variety of flours <raiseing> Delicately and highly flavered raised above the Grass, which Strikes & profumes the Sensation, and amuses the mind throws it into Conjecterng the cause of So magnificent a Senerey in a Country this Situated far removed from the Sivilised world to be enjoyed by nothing but the Buffalo Elk Deer & Bear in which it abounds & Savage Indians."

Chapter 17

Life on the River

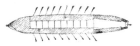

"The Musquetors are verry bad."
—William Clark, May 29th

"I have a verry Sore Throat, & am Tormented with Musquetors & Small ticks."
—William Clark, June 3rd

"The misquitoes and Ticks are noumerous & bad."
—William Clark, June 16th

"The Musquetors are beginning to be verry troublesome."
—William Clark, June 17th

"Geathered wood to make fires to Keep off the musquitor & Knats."
—William Clark, June 23rd

"The Musquitors Ticks & Knats verry troublesome."
—William Clark, June 24th

"I was Compessed to go to the woods and Combat with the Musqutors."
—William Clark, July 26th

"a butifill Breeze from the N W. this evening which would have been verry agreeable, had the Misquiters been tolerably Pacifick, but thy were rageing all night. Some about the Sise of house flais."
—William Clark, July 27th

"I Killed a Deer in the Prarie and found the Misquitors So thick & troublesome that it was disagreeable and painfull to Continue a moment Still."
—William Clark, July 27th

"The Musquitors more numerous than I ever Saw them."
—William Clark, August 3rd

"mosquitors more troublesome last night than I ever Saw them."
—William Clark, August 7th

"the Misqutors So bad in the Praries that with the assistance of a bush I could not Keep them out of my eyes."
—William Clark, August 8th

Each day brought excitement to the Corps of Discovery as the men encountered new territory, new plants and animals, and new Indians. Each day also brought a certain monotony as they fought the same river and the same insects month after month. A typical day began at first light. Breakfast was cold leftovers from the last night's dinner. After the tents and cooking gear were carefully packed in the covered sides of the keelboat, the men climbed into their familiar vessels and set off up the Missouri. About 20 men navigated the large boat. The two small boats, or pirogues, each held six to eight.

There were four ways to propel the boats. If the men were lucky, they hoisted a sail and let a favorable wind do the work. Failing that, that could row upstream or use poles to push off the bottom. The most difficult alternative was cordelling. This entailed tying a rope to the main mast and towing the boat upstream with brute force while wading alongside the muddy banks. Rowing and poling were strenuous. Cordelling was exhausting. Clark observed, "that the men Swet more than is Common from Some Cause, I think the Missouries water is the principal Cause. Those men that do not work at all will wet a Shirt in a Few minits & those who work, the Swet will run off in Streams."

Even though cordelling was arduous and slow, the men considered it "the safest and most expeditious mode of traveling, except with sails in a steady and favorable breeze." When rowing or poling the men were forced to stay out of the main current because of its' strength. This meant traveling the eddies alongside the river's edge—a dangerous place to be. The banks of the Missouri were constantly being eroded by the flow of the river. Many times the expedition witnessed the awesome spectacle of thousands of cubic yards of dirt, debris, and massive trees collapsing into the river. If they had happened to be rowing nearby at that moment, even the keelboat would have been destroyed and many men killed. In describing these collapses, Lewis later wrote that, "we have had many hairbreadth escapes from them but Providence seems to have ordered it that we have as yet sustained no loss in consequence of them."

There were other dangers. Shifting sand bars and snags could stop the boat in a heartbeat. Drifting logs, sometimes completely submerged and as large as four feet in diameter, were like icebergs ready to rip into the boat in an unobserved moment. The bowman carried a long metal tipped pole to move such dangerous obstacles out of harm's way, but the Missouri was so muddy that the bowman could often only see

x2836-08

This 1908 photograph shows a Mandan Indian standing along the banks of the Missouri River. Notice the severely undercut bank that could suddenly collapse. Photo from the Library of Congress, Prints and Photographs Division, LC-USZ-62-46989.

an inch below the water. On a good day they might make twenty miles, but mileage could be a deceptive measure of progress. Sergeant Gass complained one day that they had traveled twelve miles along an especially twisting section of the Missouri. Unfortunately, the twelve miles represented only 370 yards as the crow flies.

Not everyone traveled by water. Lewis was usually off exploring with only his dog for companionship. Drouillard would take a couple men and horses to go hunting. They rode out ahead of the boats and brought anything they shot back to the river. The hunters would then tie the carcass to a high tree branch where the sergeants on the boat would be sure to see it and the wolves wouldn't be able to take it first. Clark recorded the hunters' success each day. Drouillard would usually kill several deer each day; one day he killed six. Occasionally he would get a beaver, bear, or elk. By dinner, the famished men were ready to devour whatever fresh game was available. Once they hit buffalo country, each man would eat almost ten pounds of meat per day. The French voyagers, who had been hired to pilot one of the pirogues to the Mandan villages, complained about what they considered scanty rations. Their custom was to eat five or six times a day, which would have left little time for anything else. Clark had no patience for such requests. He noted only that the Frenchmen were "roughly rebuked." Unlike the white settlers who would follow, Lewis and Clark were careful to fully use the animals they killed. The skins were converted to clothing and moccasins. Bones were cracked to obtain the marrow. The fat was rendered and used for soup stock, soap, candles, and mosquito repellent.

Even though there was enough food to keep the men's stomachs full, they weren't eating a healthy diet. They almost never had fruits or vegetables. Their jerky was contaminated with bacteria. Little wonder then that most of the men suffered from boils and ulcers. Dysentery was another common ailment. Clark blamed the muddy water, which was surely a factor, though not the main one. Lewis kept up the bloodletting and handed out Rush's pills. The men must have dreaded visits to the doctor. The "cure" was often worse than the disease and to make matters worse it wasn't even a cure.

Every man suffered from mosquito bites. Clark struggled for words to describe just how oppressive the insects were. On August 3rd they were "more numerous" than he had ever seen. Four days later, they were even worse. On one occasion, the men were forced to tear down camp and relocate because the mosquitoes could not be endured. Elliot Coues, who edited the journals in 1893, commented that Clark was not exaggerating their discomfort. The mosquitoes truly were "troublesome." Coues noted that the mosquitoes were so thick along parts of the Missouri that they were capable of killing horses and cattle by filling their nasal passages and causing suffocation. Lewis had fortunately brought some netting for the men to sleep under. Without it, the mosquitoes would have made sleep all but impossible.

Lewis knew mosquitoes were a pest. He didn't know they were a medical calamity. No one did. Dr. Rush was investigating the causes of malaria back in Philadelphia but it would be decades before the mosquito was finally identified as the culprit. In the west, malaria was just a fact of life—something that was lived with. Lewis brought Peruvian bark to treat "bilious fevers," as he called the disease. The bark was somewhat effective in treating the symptoms but it never cured the disease entirely.

Snakes were another pest. Rattlesnakes were common. Occasionally, Lewis had to treat a man with bark for a poisonous bite. By August, Clark was pleased to report that "snakes are not plenty in this part of the Missourie." Once near a pond, the men heard a sound like a turkey gobble. The woodsman Drouillard heard the sound and told the camp that the sound came from a giant snake. In this unexplored country anything was possible. He fired his gun and the noise became even louder. Now the men were nervous. One of the Frenchmen corroborated his story. Clark recorded the incident in his journal although, luckily, the expedition never saw nor was attacked by any anacondas or boa constrictors. The closest giant snakes were thousands of miles away, but no one knew that for sure. Drouillard was probably repeating an old Indian legend, or maybe he was just having some fun with his friends.

In the evening, the sergeants would start looking for a place to camp. Islands were preferred since they were easier to defend from Indians. While the men set up camp, the cooks prepared dinner. Once they got away from the last white settlements, the hunters usually provided fresh meat. They could also rely on a steady supply of catfish. If the hunters and fisherman were unsuccessful, dinner would be provided from the stores on the keelboat. There was a three-day rotation. Day one was hominy and lard, followed by salt pork and flour, and then cornmeal and pork. Each man also received about four ounces a day from the valuable whisky supply. Lewis, Clark, and Drouillard ate separately from the other men. York was their cook.

If the men had any energy left at the end of the day, they would swap stories or dance to the music of Pierre Cruzatte's fiddle. Lewis had ordered the sergeants to write in their journals every day. Clark was also a faithful recorder. Privates Whitehouse and Frazer kept a journal. Lewis himself was the unfortunate exception. His journal entries are sporadic to say the least. He was also busy taking celestial measurements.

Lewis used the sextant and octant to measure the position of the sun and moon at specified times relative to fixed stars. He hoped that astronomers would be able to use his measurements to determine the exact longitudes and latitudes of their positions on the river. This was not a simple process. Lewis' chronometer was unreliable and cloudy nights sometimes made it impossible to take measurements.

Sentries were posted each night. Every time they were replaced the old and new guard would examine the camp for 150 yards in every direction. This vigilance was a wise precaution. Few of the Indian tribes they encountered would risk an assault on such a well-armed and alert force as the Corps of Discovery. But many tribes would happily steal horses or supplies if they decided the risk was worth the reward. The captains' military discipline insured that such a risk was never advisable.

Chapter 18

First Encounter With Indians

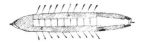

"Children. Commissioned and sent by the great Chief of the Seventeen great nations of America, we have come to inform you, as we go also to inform all the nations of red men who inhabit the borders of the Missouri, that a great council was lately held between this great chief and your old fathers the French and Spaniards. The great chief has become your only father; he is the only friend to whom you can now look for protection, or from whom you can ask favors, or receive good councils, and he will take care that you shall have no just cause to regret this change; he will serve you, & not deceive you."

--from Captain Lewis' prepared speech to the Indians,
explaining his mission.

The Corps of Discovery reached the mouth of the Platte River on July 21, 1804. This was significant for several reasons. First, they were now in Sioux territory. The expedition had been on the Missouri for almost two months

115

and had not encountered a single Indian, primarily because they had all moved to the plains to hunt buffalo. That was about to change. The eco-system was also about to change. Clark had already noted on the 15th that "the high Praries are also good land Covered with Grass entirely void of timber except what grows on the water." They were at the eastern edge of the Great Plains. From here on, Lewis would be discovering new plants and animals every few days. Most importantly, they reached the Platte several weeks ahead of an intercepting party of Spanish soldiers and Comanche Indians. This force had orders to stop the expedition, by force if necessary.

Lewis and Clark finally came across some Indians about two weeks later. They were from a combined tribe of Missouri and Oto. These Indians were both farmers and hunters. The Missouri had decided to join the Oto just a few years earlier when their population had been decimated by warfare with other tribes and smallpox. Most of the tribe, including their primary chief, Little Thief, was still on the plains hunting. A group of about a dozen warriors, accompanied by a French translator, approached the camp at sunset. The Indians fired some shots to announce their presence. The Americans fired their cannon. After this obligatory show of force, they sat down for a pleasant meeting. The Indians received some tobacco and pork. They brought some watermelons as a return gift. The group favorably impressed Private Whitehouse: "They are a handsome stout well made set of Indians & have good open Countenances, and are of a light brown colour, and have long black hair, which they do wear without cutting; and they all use paint in order to compleat their dress." The Indians agreed to return the next day for a formal council. The Missouri and Oto seemed peaceful enough. Still, Clark was an experienced Indian fighter and knew enough to be wary at all times. He ordered "every man on his Guard & ready for

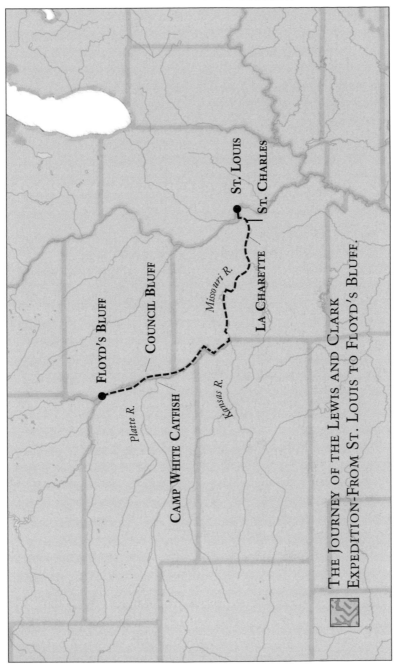

St. Louis

St. Charles

La Charette

Missouri R.

Council Bluff

Floyd's Bluff

Platte R.

Camp White Catfish

Kansas R.

The Journey of the Lewis and Clark Expedition-From St. Louis to Floyd's Bluff.

any thing."

The next morning was the first occurrence of a scene to be repeated many times. The captains put on their dress uniforms and hats. They marched the men in formation and fired a few volleys. The flag was raised. Then Lewis read a 30-minute speech that could only be described as tedious and condescending. Fortunately, the Indians had grown accustomed to such treatment from the French and Spanish. The Indians were referred to as "children" and Jefferson was now their "Great Father." The Great Father was offering both a carrot and a stick. If the tribes were peaceful to both whites and other Indians, and agreed to trade with American merchants, a permanent trading post would be established nearby. In retrospect, this sounds more like a threat than an inducement. However, the Indians needed manufactured goods, particularly guns and powder, if they were to survive against the British-supplied tribes like the Sioux. Lewis didn't leave any doubt as to the dire consequences of disobedience to the Great Father. The U.S., or the "Seventeen great nations of America," as Lewis called the states, were an irresistible force. Using powerful imagery, Lewis claimed that American "cities are as numerous as the stars of the heavens," and that the Great Father "could consume you as the fire consumes the grass of the plains."

Lewis then handed out peace medals to the major chiefs, along with a few paper certificates declaring the lesser chiefs to be friends and allies of the U.S. They then opened pre-packaged bale #30 and gave away some paint, combs, and a few clothes. After the speech, Lewis shot his air gun to the amazement of the Indians.

The Indians seemed appropriately impressed. They were glad that the Great Father was going to protect them. They would also be happy to trade with the Americans. They were a bit disappointed with the meager presents, and asked for some powder and whisky. (This was also to be a re-occurring

Captain Lewis & Clark holding a Council with the Indians.

This drawing was first published in the "Journals of Patrick Gass." The expedition dressed in their formal uniforms to meet the Indians. Picture from the Library of Congress, Prints and Photographs Division, LC-USZ-62-17372.

event.) These were the two commodities that Lewis least liked to share with Indians. He gave them a single canister of powder and a bottle of whisky. The Indians must have been somewhat pleased with the gifts, for Private Whitehouse records that the French traders never even gave them a knife for free. Lewis sent a written copy of his speech back with the Indians for Little Thief to review when he returned to camp. In his journal, Clark notes that the Missouri and Oto "are no Oreters," which is probably what the Indians would have written in their own journals about Lewis if they had had a written language. Overall, Lewis had to be pleased with his first Indian council. The tribes had been receptive. Everyone had left happy. It was also a good warm-up for the Yankton Sioux and Teton Sioux, who would be a much tougher and more important audience.

In the absence of Indians, Lewis busied himself

CHIEF RED SHIRT

The U.S. government often gave Indian chiefs medals as symbols of goodwill. This is a photograph of Chief Red Shirt at the 1903 Exposition in St. Louis wearing a President Grant peace medal. Photo from the Library of Congress, Prints and Photographs Division, LC-USZ-62-101337.

finding and describing new plants and animals. While they had been preparing for their meeting with the Missouri and Oto, Private Joseph Fields killed a badger. In trying to describe this new animal, Clark said it had the shape and size of a beaver, the head of a dog without the ears, the tail and hair of a ground hog; the "interals" (whatever those are?) were like a hogs, and the thick, loose skin reminded Clark of a bear. Lewis decided to skin and stuff the specimen for science just in case Clark's description left zoologists wondering. Within a few days, Lewis would find and describe a great egret, the least tern, and a bullsnake. His descriptions are detailed and precise. What a shame that we have no such similar writings of his first impressions of the Indians or even his observations about his own men.

At the same time the badger was killed, the hunters had also taken a small beaver alive. No group of men out camping is content without a pet. Lewis had his Newfoundland. The enlisted men decided to domesticate this beaver and make it part of the expedition. The experiment must have failed since the poor beaver is never mentioned again. There was a similar experiment back in June with a wolf cub. That time, the "pet" chewed through its rope and escaped.

On August 8th, the men were pushing the boat upriver when they encountered an unusual sight. The surface of the water was covered with white feathers in a ribbon 60-70 yards wide, yet no birds were in sight. This ribbon of feathers continued along the river for three miles. They found the source of the feathers on a sand bar attached to a small island. It was a flock of pelicans, "the number of which would if estimated appear almost incredible." The pelican was not unknown. Lewis had read about them but never seen one. He didn't try to guess their numbers but noted that the flock covered several acres. Lewis decided to procure a specimen. Without even bothering to aim his rifle, he shot into the birds and killed one. He then meticulously described its physical characteristics, habitat, and nesting habits. By careful measurement, he found that the pouch in the pelican's beak held five gallons of water. His observations are insightful for an amateur scientist. The same day he wrote that they had heard katydids for the first time on July 27th, and gave the latitude.

There were also new fish. The expedition's chief fisherman, Silas Goodrich, was catching gigantic catfish. Each fish rendered nearly a quart of oil. When the pelicans fled from the boats, they left behind several species of fish Lewis had never seen before. The biggest fish story of all happened the next week. On August 14th, the hunters were unable to kill any meat. To feed the men, Captain Clark took a small group and went fishing in a beaver pond about a mile from camp. Clark rigged a net across the creek and caught 308 fish as well as some shrimp—not very sporting but quite effective. Captain Lewis took another group the next day and more than doubled Clark's take.

They were now in the territory of the Omaha Indians. The captains wanted to let this tribe know of their new Great Father but no Omahas could be found. They were off hunting buffalo. Had the expedition taken place just a few years earlier, the Omahas might well have been present to greet the expedition—and to plunder their supplies. Led by a powerful chief named Blackbird, they had been the pirates of the Missouri. Any trader unfortunate enough to come across the Omahas could expect to be attacked or forced to pay a large toll. Blackbird was equally ruthless to his own people. He obtained arsenic from the traders, and any member of his tribe foolish enough to oppose his will was likely to end up poisoned. Disaster struck the Omahas in the winter of 1799. Smallpox decimated their population. Panic set in. They burned their villages. According to Clark, "they put their wives & Children to Death with a view of their all going together to Some better Countrey." This marked the end of the Omaha threat to white traders. Four years later, their society was still in disarray. Clark noted that these Indians have "no houses no Corn or any thing more than the graves of their ancestors to attach them to the old Village." Clark left a U.S. flag on Blackbird's burial mound and proceeded on.

Private Francis Labiche returned to camp on August 17th. He was one of the men who had had accompanied Drouillard on his mission to capture the deserters Reed and LaLiberte. This reconnaissance party had been gone for ten days and the captains had begun to worry. Labiche explained that Drouillard was camped just a few miles away. They had captured both men, although LaLiberte had tricked them and escaped again. Reed was still in custody. They had also met up with some of the Oto and Missouri chiefs who had been gone hunting buffalo during their previous council meeting two weeks earlier. Drouillard had convinced these Indians, including the main chief, Little Thief, to return and meet with Lewis and Clark. However, the Otos were not ready to march into camp just yet.

A short time earlier two Missouri warriors had snuck into the camp of the Omahas to steal some horses. They had both been captured and killed. These deaths had sparked a war between the Omahas and combined Missouri/Oto tribes. There may have been other causes. Sergeant Ordway wrote that the Otos would sometimes harvest the corn of the Omahas while they were away on the buffalo hunt. Little Thief and the other chiefs had no intention of meeting with the captains until they were sure there were no hostile Indians around. Labiche had instructions to fire the cannon if no Omahas were in camp, which they did the next morning.

Around 10:00 A.M., Drouillard brought in the Indians and Private Reed. The expedition shared their breakfast with the Otos and proceeded immediately to the court-martial of Reed. Desertion was a capital offense and there was little doubt as to Reed's guilt. The captains faced a difficult decision. Should they hang Reed? They had already given Drouillard permission to shoot him if necessary. Reed had lied, stole valuable supplies, and slowed the expedition while Drouillard chased him down. Worse, he had set a dangerous precedent. They could certainly not allow desertions, and a swift, severe punishment would deter any future occurrences. By nature, Clark was a merciful commander but a series of disciplinary problems over the past few months threatened the success of their mission. Reed's desertion was the most serious offense. The insubordination had to end here.

Reed spoke to the court. He admitted his guilt and "requested we would be as favourable with him as we Could consistently with our Oathes." This was probably the smartest defense Reed could muster. If he had acted the least bit defiant, or made excuses for his behavior, or shown himself in any way to be a possible source of contention within the camp, Lewis and Clark would have had no alternative but to execute him. As it was, he stood contrite and trusted to the captains' mercy. To hang him now might be perceived as excessive by the men.

The captains decided to let him live. He was expelled from the Corps of Discovery. He would continue on the expedition but would not be allowed the privilege of carrying a gun or posting guard duty. When Corporal Warfington returned to St. Louis in the spring with the French voyagers, Reed would return too. He would also run the gauntlet four times. This meant that Reed would be forced to run past all the men of the expedition. Each would have a willow switch or a ramrod. In total, Reed would receive around 500 lashes, just about the maximum a man could endure without dying.

The Indians watched the proceedings with interest, but when the sentence was explained to them they were shocked. The Otos would never humiliate a warrior in such a way. They would allow him an honorable death instead. The captains explained the necessity of the punishment. Men like

Reed were a danger to the Indians. They could cause much mischief with their lies and deceptions. After the justification, Little Thief and the other chiefs accepted the propriety of the gauntlet and witnessed the procedure.

The day also happened to be Captain Lewis' birthday. In celebration, the men received an extra ration of whisky. Cruzatte played his fiddle, and the soldiers danced until almost midnight.

The next morning Lewis prepared to make his standard Indian presentation a second time. There was one important difference. One of the Missouri chiefs, Big Horse, arrived at camp completely naked. This was a brilliant negotiating tactic. Here was Lewis, in his gaudy full dress uniform and cocked hat, reading a formal message from the President of the United States to a naked Indian. He had to be unnerved. After the recitation, the Indians were ready to reply. Little Thief was willing to be peaceful. This was a somewhat self-serving position. Like the Omahas, the Otos had also been hit with smallpox. They were vulnerable to other tribes. It was to their advantage to have an American-enforced peace. They asked the captains to stay and negotiate a treaty between them and the Omaha. They asked if Labiche could stay and help broker a peace with the Shawnee. The captains were unable to comply with either request. Resolving centuries of warfare between Indian tribes was not their primary objective. They could not wait and they could not spare any men.

Big Horse now had a practical request for Captain Lewis: "I came here naked and must return home naked. if I have Something to give the young men I can prevent their going to war. You want to make peace with all, It is good we want Something to give my men at home. I am a pore man, and cant quiet without means, a Spoon ful of your milk will qui[e]t all." Big Horse was not referring to cow's milk, which the captains didn't have anyway. He meant whisky. Again, the captains refused. If they gave the Otos a barrel of whisky they would have rebellion among their own men to worry about. They also surely realized that if, on this occasion, alcohol served as an impediment rather than an accelerant to fighting, it would likely be the first time. Still, Big Horse did have a valid point. Without raiding or fighting, how would the men provide for their families? How would the young men prove themselves as warriors and chiefs?

Lewis and Clark started distributing gifts. There was a little tobacco, a few beads, combs, and some clothing. The Indians knew the keelboat was full of trade goods. Why were the captains so stingy? Big Horse received a peace medal to match the one given to Little Thief. The other Indians, whom the captains deemed lesser chiefs, received a paper certificate verifying their status as a friend and ally of the United States. The Otos were not impressed. A chief named Big Blue Eyes handed back the valueless certificate. Clark was irritated at this disrespect. He "rebuked them verry roughly for having in object goods and not peace with their neighbors." Big Blue Eyes asked for his certificate back. Clark refused at first and then relented after the Indian made a "plausible excuse." Ultimately, the council ended in disappointment for both sides. The Indians couldn't understand why the white men commanded them to be peaceful, and then failed to provide any means to achieve peace. By the end of the day, Clark complained that "those people became extreemly troublesom to us begging Whisky & little articles." They gave the Indians a dram of whisky and sent them home. At least there was no fighting between them. The Oto, Missouri, and Omaha were not equipped to fight such a well-armed force. A few miles upstream, their more powerful Sioux neighbors might be less hospitable.

There was a more immediate problem. Sergeant Floyd had become violently ill. Three weeks earlier, during the first meeting with the Otos, he had been dancing too vigorously. When his turn came for guard duty he collapsed on a sand bar.

Gass described Floyd's ailment as the "cramp colic." Floyd quickly recovered and was able to participate in the strenuous duties of the expedition. There is no record in his journal, or the others, of any further symptoms until August 19th. Clark spent that entire night nursing Floyd but "could get nothing to Stay on his Stomach a moment."

The next day brought no improvement. Clark ordered the boats ashore so they could make a warm bath for Floyd. Before the bath could be prepared, Floyd told Clark, "I am going away. I want you to write me a letter." It was his last request. Clark praised him highly: "Floyd Died with a great deel of Composure. This man at all times gave us proofs of his firmness and Deturmined resolution to doe Service to his Countrey and honor to himself." The Corps of Discovery buried their first casualty that same day on top of a high round hill they named Sergeant Floyds Bluff. Lewis made a speech at his grave.

The conventional wisdom among historians has been that Floyd died of a ruptured appendix. Dr. Bruce C. Paton, who wrote a history of the expedition from a medical perspective, concludes that appendicitis was "possible, but very unlikely." Death from appendicitis takes several days or weeks and includes regular, painful symptoms. If Floyd's own journal can be trusted, he was a healthy man who contracted some type of catastrophic ailment and was dead within 24 hours. The suddenness of his death, coupled with the constant vomiting and diarrhea, suggest some type of massive abdominal infection. There was definitely opportunity to be infected. The men were drinking water straight from the river. They were eating whatever plants and animals they could find along the way. Certainly the food was not always prepared in a sanitary manner. Still, few bacteria could act so quickly and lethally. According to Dr. Paton, Floyd could have also died from a perforated duodenal ulcer, a ruptured aneurysm, or an obstructed blood supply. Given the scant information that Clark recorded about Floyd's symptoms, the exact cause of his death will probably remain a mystery.

If Floyd had been treated by the best doctor of his day-- probably Dr. Rush--he would have fared no better. Dr. Rush would have done exactly what Clark did: provide the patient with Rush's pills and let some blood. The bloodletting would have diluted his strength. The pills only made the suffering worse.

The night of Floyd's death, the expedition camped at a small river, which they also named for Floyd. Two days later, the men voted on a replacement. Patrick Gass was chosen and promoted to sergeant. Problems continued. The same day that Gass was elected, Lewis discovered a "clear Soft Substance" on a high bluff. Ever the curious scientist, he performed some experiments to determine what it was. He pounded it, smelled it, and tasted it. It turned out to be arsenic. This time Rush's pills proved quite effective in ridding Lewis' body of a lethal poison.

Within a few days of Lewis' mishap, one of the hunters, George Shannon, disappeared. John Colter went after him but could find no trace. Drouillard also searched for him. Again, he had no success. The captains did not suspect desertion. Shannon was a trusted member of the party. They were worried about Indians. The Yankton Sioux were just a few miles away. This was a critical moment for the Corps of Discovery. They had just lost one of their leaders by death. There were two deserters; one disgraced, the other still missing. Lewis was recovering from a near fatal self-poisoning. Now, a valuable hunter was lost in hostile Sioux territory. They were at reduced strength and morale, and unbeknown to them they were being pursued by a battalion of Spanish soldiers. Within a few days they would undoubtedly meet their first band of Sioux warriors. Jefferson had explicitly instructed Lewis to open favorable trading relations with the Sioux. They were the most powerful tribe on the upper Missouri and the key to establishing a U.S. trading empire. They were also allies of the British and had no reason to cast their lot with the young, American republic. Lewis and Clark both realized that their next meeting with the Indians could mark the expedition's greatest success or its greatest failure.

Bibliography

Ambrose, Stephen E.
*Undaunted Courage: Meriwether Lewis, Thomas Jefferson,
    and the Opening of the American West.*
New York: Simon & Schuster, 1996.

Ambrose, Stephen E.
Lewis & Clark: Voyage of Discovery.
National Geographic Society, 1998.

Ambrose, Stephen E.
To America: Personal Reflections of an Historian.
New York: Simon & Schuster, 2002.

Bakeless, John.
*Background to Glory: The Life of
    George Rogers Clark.*
Lincoln: University of Nebraska Press, 1957.

Bakeless, John.
Lewis and Clark: Partners in Discovery.
New York: William Morrow & Company, 1947.

Clarke, Charles G.
The Men of the Lewis & Clark Expedition.
Lincoln: University of Nebraska Press, 1970.

DeVoto, Bernard.
Across the Wide Missouri.
New York: Houghton Mifflin Company, 1947.

DeVoto, Bernard, Editor.
The Journals of Lewis and Clark.
Boston: Houghton Mifflin Company, 1953.

Duncan, Dayton and Burns, Ken,
Lewis & Clark: The Journey of the Corps of Discovery.
New York: Alfred A Knopf, 1997.

Ferris, Robert G.,
Lewis and Clark.
Washington D.C.: National Park Service, 1975.

Jackson, Donald.
Thomas Jefferson & the Stony Mountains:
Exploring the West from Monticello.
Urbana: University of Illinois Press, 1981.

Jackson, Donald.
Letters of the Lewis and Clark Expedition.
Urbana: University of Illinois Press, 1978.

MacGregor, Carol Lynn, Editor.
The Journals of Patrick Gass.
Missoula: Mountain Press Publishing, 1997.

Moulton, Gary, Editor.
The Journals of the Lewis & Clark Expedition
    11 Volumes
Lincoln: University of Nebraska Press, 1986-1997

Paton, Bruce C.
Lewis and Clark: Doctors in the Wilderness.
Golden, Colorado: Fulcrum Publishing, 2001.

Thorp, Daniel B,
Lewis and Clark: An American Journey.
New York: Michael Friedman Publishing Group, 1998.

Additional Apricot Press Books

'The Wayside Bookshop'

Lewis & Clark is $9.95 US.
All other books are $6.95 US.

'The Truth About Life' Humor Books

Apricot Press Order Form

Book Title	Quantity	x	Cost / Book	=	Total
_____	_____		_____		_____
_____	_____		_____		_____
_____	_____		_____		_____
_____	_____		_____		_____
_____	_____		_____		_____
_____	_____		_____		_____
_____	_____		_____		_____
_____	_____		_____		_____

Do not send Cash. Mail check or money order to:
**Apricot Press   P.O. Box 1611
American Fork, Utah   84003**
Telephone 801-756-0456
Allow 3 weeks for delivery.

**Quantity discounts available.
Call us for more information.**
9 a.m. - 5 p.m. MST

Sub Total =

Shipping =   **$2.00**

Tax 8.5% =

Total Amount
Enclosed =

Shipping Address

Name:

Street:

City: State:

Zip Code:

Telephone:

Email: